JUBILATE AGNO

CHRISTOPHER SMART

JUBILATE AGNO

RE-EDITED FROM
THE ORIGINAL MANUSCRIPT
WITH AN INTRODUCTION
AND NOTES BY

W. H. BOND
Curator of Manuscripts
at the Houghton Library, Harvard

GREENWOOD PRESS, PUBLISHERS
WESTPORT, CONNECTICUT

The Library of Congress cataloged this book as follows:

Smart, Christopher, 1722–1771.
    Jubilate Agno. Re-edited from the original manuscript
with an introd. and notes by W. H. Bond. New York, Greenwood Press ₍1969₎

    171 p. 23 cm. 8.50

    "Originally published in 1954."

    I. Bond, William Henry, 1915–   ed. II. Title.

PR3687.S7J8 1969   821'.6   72–90159
SBN 8371–2331–3   MARC

Library of Congress   70 ₍4₎

Originally published in 1954 by Harvard University Press

Reprinted with the permission of Rupert-Hart-Davis Ltd.,
London

Reprinted in 1969 by Greenwood Press, Inc.,
51 Riverside Avenue, Westport, Conn. 06880

Library of Congress catalog card number 72-90159
ISBN 0-8371-2331-3

Printed in the United States of America

10 9 8 7 6 5 4 3

FOR
HYDER EDWARD ROLLINS

CONTENTS

INTRODUCTION 11

THE TEXT AND ITS ANNOTATION 25

ACKNOWLEDGEMENTS 26

ABBREVIATIONS 27

FRAGMENT A 29

FRAGMENT B1 39

FRAGMENT B2 91

FRAGMENT C 121

FRAGMENT D 143

TEXTUAL NOTES 165

CONVERSION TABLE 171

INTRODUCTION

I

CHRISTOPHER SMART'S *Jubilate Agno* is surely one of the great oddities of English poetry. But it is not merely a curiosity. It commands attention for many reasons, as its discoverer and first editor, Mr. William Force Stead, was at pains to demonstrate. Not only does it contain many phrases and passages of striking beauty and power, but it also provides the key necessary to understand and explain its author's masterwork, *A Song to David*. And now that the original plan of its construction has been recovered, *Jubilate Agno* becomes at once somewhat less mad and considerably more revealing.

The myth of Smart as a one-poem author, a talent that blazed for one brief moment only in an otherwise dull career, is now thoroughly discredited. The true worth of much that he wrote both before and after *A Song to David* has come to be properly appreciated. But no one can deny that the poet who went into the madhouse in 1756 was very different from the poet who emerged seven years later, and *Jubilate Agno* is the crucial document for an understanding of his transformation. Some consideration of his life and works is necessary if we are to see this extraordinary composition in its proper context.

Christopher Smart was born in Kent in 1722. His mother was a Welsh-woman, as he proudly records in *Jubilate*; his father, Peter Smart, was steward of the estates of William, Viscount Vane. Smart's first love was the daughter of Vane's nephew Henry, the Anne Hope who appears several times in *Jubilate*; frequent references also occur in the poem to Shipbourne, Fairlawn, Raby Castle, and Staindrop, all places associated with the Vanes.

Smart was a premature baby and a delicate child, and the cordials habitually administered to him may well have developed the taste for stimulants which later helped to ruin him. He was evidently both bright and likeable, and was treated virtually as a member of the family by his father's patrons. When Peter Smart died in 1733, the widow sent her son to Durham School, and young Christopher was always warmly received at Raby Castle, the local seat of Henry Vane, now Lord Barnard. When at the age of seventeen Smart proceeded to Pembroke Hall, Cambridge, he still enjoyed the family's protection. The Duchess of Cleveland, Lord Barnard's mother-in-law, presented him with an annuity of forty pounds. This helped support him at the University and later served to postpone the wreck of his affairs.

At Cambridge Smart proved an excellent classical scholar. Meanwhile his reputation as a poet grew. To the facile vein of occasional verse which he had essayed with some success even as a schoolboy, he added more serious work in both Latin and English. By 1742 his studies had won him in open competition the title of "Scholar of the University," while his growing claim to the title of University Poet may be seen in the ode which he composed in 1743 for the four hundredth anniversary of the founding of Pembroke. He read, wrote, and taught, and in 1745 was elected Fellow of Pembroke; his university career seemed assured. But the financial spectre which was to haunt the rest of his life now appeared. In 1746 the family fortunes, never vigorous, suffered a decline, and by the next year Smart was in serious difficulties. His friends and admirers rallied to his support, and he was saved for the moment; but he did not abate the excesses which had brought about his crisis. By the autumn of 1747 his creditors took action and the University deprived him of his offices; but still Cambridge worked to save her poet, whose drunkenness might possibly be reformed, and he was reinstated for the year 1748–1749. At the end of that time he left Cambridge for London and the life of a professional writer. His Fellowship at Pembroke Hall was retained for some years, so that he was eligible to compete for the Seatonian Prize for religious poetry. This prize was first offered for competition in 1750, and was won by Smart. All told he carried off the Seatonian Prize five times in the first six years of its history.

In London Smart plunged into a life of feverish activity. He became one of John Newbery's stable of literary hacks (Goldsmith was another at a later date), editing and writing the greater part of two periodicals. *The Student* and *The Midwife* are crammed with his pieces, under his own name and a variety of fantastic pseudonyms. It is impossible to determine his responsibility for other publications from Newbery's prolific shop; one suspects that he did a good deal of unacknowledged work.[1] Meanwhile he became acquainted with Jonathan Tyers, the proprietor of Vauxhall Gardens, and wrote songs for him which were set by William Boyce, Thomas Arne, and various lesser composers. Through Arne he met Dr. Charles Burney, father of the author of *Evelina*, and a loyal friend in Smart's later troubles. He also worked with Richard Rolt and Arthur Murphy, and fought in various Grub Street skirmishes by their side. When Smart attacked the notorious "Sir" John Hill in *The Hilliad*, it was Murphy who collaborated on the "Notes Variorum."

Now Smart's private life took a new turn: he began courting his publisher's step-daughter, Anna Maria Carnan, and some time in 1752 they were married

[1] A book that may well contain Smart's work, at least in an editorial capacity, is *The Wonders of Nature and Art*, 6 vol. (London: J. Newbery, 1750). The compilation of such a compendium of travel, natural history, and geography, might help to explain Smart's exploration of various obscure fields of learning. It contains references to many natural objects also mentioned in *Jubilate Agno*.

INTRODUCTION

—secretly, so that his Pembroke fellowship should not lapse. A year later the secret was out, and Smart's official connection with Pembroke was severed. It is a good indication of his high reputation as a poet that the University interpreted its rules most leniently so that he could still compete for the Seatonian Prize. He had no entry ready in 1754, but in 1755 he submitted a poem once more, and took his fifth and final prize. At the other end of the scale was Mother Midnight's Oratory, a series of wild tavern-entertainments into which Smart flung himself wholeheartedly as both performer and writer. Thus his work cut across every shade of the literary spectrum; he was ready to try any variety of writing provided it promised some return.

But all this activity, all the eminence of the Seatonian contests and the notoriety of squabbles in Grub Street, was taking him nowhere. Marriage does not seem to have had a settling influence on Smart; in fact, his continued tippling may have been a refuge from the financial and other burdens attendant on family life. The strain of working at such a pace told on his rather fragile health. There is evidence of a breakdown or two before the catastrophe of 1756. His "Hymn to the Supreme Being," published in that year, commemorates his recovery from one such attack. Its dedicatory note to Dr. Robert James says that this was the third occasion when James had "rescued me from the grave."

At the same time, Smart was finding Newbery's yoke more and more galling. In 1755 he and Rolt moved to break away, contracting with the booksellers Gardner and Allen to write a monthly periodical called *The Universal Visiter*, and to write nothing similar for anyone else for the term of ninety-nine years. This is the notorious contract so roundly denounced by Dr. Johnson; however, it was filled with loopholes and any party to it might withdraw at short notice, so it was by no means as bad as Johnson thought.

The periodical began to appear in February, 1756. Soon Smart fell ill, and after three months wrote no more for it. For a while loyal friends, including Johnson, filled in for him. But Smart did not recover; his connection with *The Universal Visiter* ceased, and the first part of his career came to an abrupt end. From 1756 until early in 1763 he was under some degree of restraint almost continuously, either privately or in one of the large public institutions. Delicate health, drink, and a growing religious mania apparently combined to make him obnoxious to family and friends, and incapable of managing his own affairs.

The history of his confinement is by no means clear, and only one definite record of it has been discovered. On 6 May 1757 Smart was admitted to St. Luke's Hospital for the insane on the recommendation of Francis Gosling, to be discharged a year later, uncured. It is evident that he must have been in some asylum or other for a considerable period after this. His own remarks in *Jubilate Agno* are fairly conclusive on this point, and Fanny Burney later recorded that he had been twice confined. Some of the fellow-inmates he named in *Jubilate* are known to have been in Bethlehem Hospital, but no record survives of his confinement there. Possibly he was registered under an assumed name to avoid embarrassing his family; if so, his fate was well known to his contemporaries. Many of them, such as Johnson and Burney, are known to have visited him, and at least one theatrical benefit was given for him. It is an annoying coincidence that none of his visitors troubled to mention the place of his confinement.

Here, where his career came to a full stop, it is appropriate to enquire what manner of poet Smart was as he stood on the threshold of the madhouse. In his own phrase, he was "a man who has made poetry, perhaps, too much the business of his life." [1] The principal evidences of his accomplishment are to be seen in the five Seatonian poems, the *Poems on Several Occasions* of 1752, *The Hilliad*, and the contributions to *The Student* and *The Midwife*. These pieces cannot be dismissed as inconsequential, but despite flashes of a real poetic fire there is not much to be found in them of any outstanding merit. Smart was technically proficient in almost any kind of verse he attempted, from the solemn religious vein to the most gay and uninhibited burlesque, yet as to substance his work was almost entirely derivative. From the competent blank verse of the Seatonian poems, virtually unencumbered by original thought, to the lively fables in the manner of Gay, there is little that might not have been written by many a clever young man of his day. Unquestionably Smart enjoyed a considerable reputation. But even with the *cachet* of the Seatonian Prize, it was a reputation more for ability and promise than for solid achievement. His equipment was well above the common run, but he had yet to find the theme for its employment or to strike the note he was peculiarly endowed to sustain. Nor was he likely to do so in the course of such an existence as had fallen to his lot. Many a promising talent among Smart's contemporaries was exhausted like his in the turmoil of Grub Street: his acquaintances Charles Churchill and Robert Lloyd, for example. The constant exploitation of his gifts for rapid composition and facile imitation, the eternal necessity to scribble merely to survive, might never have permitted him to pause, take stock, and evolve that mastery of structure and that combination of benevolence and moral fervour expressed in striking phrase which are the particular glories of his best work.

His breakdown brought this turbulent and aimless career to a halt. In seven years of restraint—and much of the time he was probably no more insane than many a man outside the asylum—he contemplated his past life and present condition, he worked out a poetic theory and a personal philosophy, and he experimented with form and style in a manner wholly original

[1] In the introduction to his prose Horace of 1756.

and unconventional. He was forced to give up the world, and in so doing he found himself. The surviving fragments of *Jubilate Agno*, written during those years, are the only records we have of the experiments and the probings of intellect and spirit with which Smart occupied his time. When he emerged from the shadows his days of imitation were over. Within a few months he published *A Song to David*, the mature product of his thought and labours. It was a poem unlike any he had ever published before, which is to say that it was quite outside the comfortable channels of eighteenth-century verse. It is no wonder that his contemporaries took one look at *A Song to David* and continued to regard its author as a madman.

Jubilate Agno will be considered in detail later; meantime, it is proper to complete its frame and glance at the closing years of Smart's life. *A Song to David*, which came out in the Spring of 1763, was not a success. Some readers, like Boswell, glimpsed at least a few of its beauties; more, like Mason, concluded from it that Smart was as mad as ever. Mason's view prevailed, and the Rev. Christopher Hunter saw fit to omit the poem altogether from the collected edition of 1791. Two other small pamphlets of verse were published later in 1763: *Poems by Mr. Smart* and *Poems on Several Occasions*. Smart was trying desperately to support himself by these publications: all three were "Printed for the Author" and all bore his autograph signature at the end by way of authentication. The critical response was discouraging, as indeed it was for all his later works. His friends were too ready to be saddened, and his enemies too eager to be pleased, by discovering signs of madness in everything he did. He quarrelled with his critics, and thereafter received worse reviews than ever. It became virtually impossible for him to obtain a fair hearing, and consequently to sell his writings; his last years were an unending struggle against impossible odds. The sweetness of spirit which distinguishes much of this work becomes the more astonishing when viewed against the background of bitter circumstance which closed in upon him.

In 1764 his oratorio *Hannah*, with music by John Worgan, was performed at the King's Theatre, Haymarket, and another pamphlet of verses appeared, *Ode to the . . . Earl of Northumberland*. Next year came the long-heralded paraphrase of the *Psalms*, which included his cycle of hymns for the Christian year and a second appearance of the *Song to David*. Its subscription books had been open since 1762, and its imposing list of patrons reveals how many persons of greater or less eminence still interested themselves in the poet. A second publication in the same year was a verse-translation of Phaedrus, a piece of hack-work done for Dodsley.

The verse-translation of Horace, in four handsome volumes, followed in 1767. It was Smart's amends for the prose trot he had produced to order eleven years before, and like the *Psalms* it is a thoroughly mature work whose worth has only recently come to be appreciated. The hymns and the Biblical and Horatian paraphrases are only less excellent than the *Song to David* in their mastery of form and texture, and in the vigour and unexpected felicity of their language. The clever but conventional versifier of the early years was indeed transformed.[1]

In 1768 came another oratorio, *Abimelech*, with music by Samuel Arnold, and a versification of the *Parables of Our Lord and Saviour Jesus Christ*, dedicated to the young son of Bonnell Thornton. The last publication of all, *Hymns for the Amusement of Children*, came out late in 1770 when the shades of the prison were closing about him.

During most of these later years Smart had a room near the Cockpit overlooking St. James's Park. There he was visited by Dr. John Hawkesworth in October 1764, and from there he addressed a begging letter to George Colman in February 1766. A legal document of July 1769, refers to him as "Christopher Smart of Chealsea," but when and why he moved from St. James's Park is not known. Perhaps he wished to be nearer the Vauxhall headquarters of the Tyers family. His life seems to have been quiet and somewhat retired, though he sometimes called on old friends. He had broken entirely with his family, and pointedly changed the subject when Dr. Hawkesworth tried to broach the question of a reconciliation with them.

It became increasingly obvious that Smart's attempts to live by his pen were doomed to failure, and at least one notable effort was made to save him. In April 1766 the King promised him the next place as Poor Pensioner of St. George's, Windsor, but no vacancy occurred in time to benefit him. His fortunes steadily declined, accelerated by a return of his old disorders. On 26 April 1770 he was arrested for debt on complaint of one James Bright and confined in King's Bench Prison. The case came to trial and a judgement against Smart was signed on 11 February 1771, and he was recommitted to prison in default of payment. His brother-in-law, Thomas Carnan, and his old friend, Dr. Charles Burney, are said to have secured the liberty of the Rules for him, but he never emerged to freedom again. On 20 May 1771 he died in prison.

II

The autograph manuscript of *Jubilate Agno* has had a curious history. That it should have survived at all appears to be due to a remarkable coincidence: nothing less than the madness of another poet, William Cowper. Cowper's affliction and its cure formed the subject of much discussion and correspondence between two of his friends, William Hayley (later his biographer), and the Rev. Thomas Carwardine. Evidently Smart's manu-

---

[1] The most perceptive modern criticism of Smart's work is to be found in the introduction and notes to Robert Brittain's edition of *Poems by Christopher Smart* (Princeton, 1950).

script came to their attention and was regarded by them as a kind of case-study in poetic mania. It remained in Carwardine's hands and became a part of the family papers, eventually coming into the possession of his great-grandson, Colonel W. G. Carwardine Probert.

In Colonel Probert's library the manuscript was seen by William Force Stead, who quickly perceived its interest and importance. Stead obtained permission to publish it, and devoted many hours of painstaking research to the compilation of exhaustive explanatory notes. His edition, *Rejoice in the Lamb: A Song from Bedlam* (a title devised by him and not by Smart), appeared in 1939. A few years later, the manuscript was acquired from Colonel Probert by the Harvard College Library, where it is now preserved.

The manuscript has not come down to us intact. As I shall presently show, what survives is only a series of fragments, representing somewhat less than half of the poem as Smart wrote it. Nothing is known of the fate of the missing portions. In his edition, Stead attempted to arrange the fragments chronologically; but he and those who have since worked on the poem failed to grasp the secret of its original structure. Yet it is possible to establish with a high degree of probability the original form and extent of the poem, and the present edition offers for the first time a full text of the fragments arranged as Smart evidently intended.[1] I have dealt with the problem of reconstructing the poem elsewhere in some detail,[2] and I shall therefore limit myself here to a briefer account.

At the outset it should be emphasized that there is no evidence that Smart ever actually contemplated the publication of *Jubilate Agno*. I shall have more to say about this when discussing the stages through which its composition passed. To begin with, it is enough to note that he never systematically revised any portion of it for the press. A few revisions and insertions do appear sporadically, and these are recorded in the textual notes to this edition, but there are many points exhibiting defects which the most careless author should have corrected in reviewing his work. Indeed, on these grounds alone *Jubilate Agno* has something of the appearance of a discarded experiment.

The poem is closely written on both sides of a series of folio leaves. There are ten single leaves and three pairs of conjunct leaves, a total of thirty-two pages. The text falls into two obvious divisions, the *Let* and the *For* sections. Every verse in the *Let* section (except the first two on the page numbered "1" by Smart) begins with the word *Let*; every verse in the *For* section (with one exception) begins with the word *For*. No *For* verses occur on any leaf

---

[1] Seventy pairs of matching verses from Fragment B were printed from an advance typescript of my edition in W. H. Auden and N. H. Pearson, *Poets of the English Language* (New York, 1950; London, 1952), III, 555–567.

[2] "Christopher Smart's *Jubilate Agno*," *Harvard Library Bulletin*, IV (Winter, 1950), 34–52.

INTRODUCTION

or conjunct pair of leaves in the *Let* section, and *vice versa*. Every page of the manuscript bears in the lower right corner a catchword in Smart's hand; the sole exception is what is obviously the last page of the *Let* section, containing only eight verses, and about three-quarters blank. In every case, the catchword on a *Let* page is *Let*, and on a *For* page it is *For*. Obviously the author intended the *Let* and *For* sections to be physically distinct. A further peculiarity is the frequent occurrence of dates in the text, dates which apparently record the time of composition of the verses in which they appear. These are of great help in attempting to determine the original arrangement.

The *Let* section consists of three double folios and three single leaves. The first page of each double folio bears a numeral in Smart's hand in its upper left corner preceding the first verse of text; these are 1, 10, and 11. One of the single leaves is similarly numbered 3, and one of the remaining single folios was demonstrably once conjugate with it. Dates in the remaining unnumbered single folio prove it to belong somewhere approximately midway between double folio 3 and double folio 10. The *Let* section comes to a conclusion on the fourth page of double folio 11. These facts lead to the assumption that the *Let* section was originally written on a series of eleven double folios, or forty-four pages, of which four and one-half double folios or eighteen pages survive.

Seven single leaves of *For* verses survive, of which three are numbered 3, 4, and 5. Three of the remaining leaves can be shown to have been conjugate with them, and thus the fragments as reconstituted make up double folios 3, 4, and 5 complete, with a single unnumbered leaf not associated with any other. Further, the text of the three consecutively numbered double folios runs on without a break. Dates in the odd leaf show that it belongs to a somewhat later period than double folio 5. We shall return to the question of the original length of the *For* section.

Although the *Let* and the *For* sections are physically distinct, their content is intimately related. The dates show that parts, at least, of the two sections were written concurrently; and when the *Let* double folio 3 is placed beside the *For* double folio 3, the most remarkable congruence appears. The four pages of *Let* text contain respectively 70, 80, 71, and 74 verses; so do the corresponding pages of *For* text. And, at least for a considerable portion, each *For* verse is in some manner and degree a response to the corresponding *Let* verse. A similar physical congruence exists between the two unnumbered single leaves of *Let* and *For* verses, although their content does not agree so well. It seems likely that the entire poem was constructed in this manner, with a line-for-line correspondence between the *Let* and *For* verses. At any rate, it was so begun and it so continued through the greater part of its length.

The defects of the manuscript necessitate its arrangement as a series of fragments, as follows:

18

INTRODUCTION

FRAGMENT A

113 lines of *Let* verses only, comprising the whole text of *Let* double folio 1. The corresponding *For* verses are wanting. Neither the *Let* nor the *For* verses of double folio 2 survive.

FRAGMENT B1

Let and *For* double folios 3, complete; each containing 295 verses, and printed on facing pages to show their parallelism.[1]

FRAGMENT B2

For double folios 4 and 5, comprising 475 verses which continue without a break the *For* verses in Fragment B1. They are numbered 296–770 to indicate this continuity. The corresponding *Let* verses are wanting.

FRAGMENT C

Both the *Let* and *For* verses of double folios 6, 7, 8, and 9 are wanting except for the matched pair of *Let* and *For* leaves. These are unnumbered and presumably the second leaves of what were originally double folios. Dates in March 1761 place this fragment after Fragments A, B1 and B2 (whose latest date is in June 1760) and before Fragment D (whose earliest date is in July 1762). The complementary passages each contain 162 verses, which are here printed on facing pages as in Fragment B1.

FRAGMENT D

Let double folios 10 and 11, comprising 237 consecutive verses. The corresponding *For* verses are wanting, if indeed Smart ever composed them. Returning to the question of the original extent of the *For* verses, we can now say with confidence that they ran beyond Fragment C (since the last *For* verse of C does not appear to be a conclusion), and they may possibly have continued in line-for-line relation with the *Let* verses to the end of Fragment D. Fragment C belongs most probably to double folio 7 or 8; therefore at the very least there must have been just over twenty-eight pages of *For* verses, and at most forty-four pages.

---

[1] In my article in the *Harvard Library Bulletin*, Fragments B1 and B2 were designated as B and B′, respectively.

19

INTRODUCTION

III

What was Smart trying to do in *Jubilate Agno*? Fortunately, his purpose is reasonably clear; and his method and attack, as they altered with the passage of time, can at least be guessed at.

In the first place, *Jubilate Agno* represents an attempt to adapt to English verse some of the principles of Hebrew verse as expounded by Bishop Robert Lowth in his pioneering study, *De sacra poesi Hebraeorum*, first published in 1753. Putting its theological content to one side, Lowth examined the Bible as a work of literature, and devoted a good deal of discussion to the rules governing its poetry. Smart certainly knew Lowth's book, and was on familiar terms with Lowth himself; in fact, Smart's family cited his friendship with Lowth after his release from the asylum as an indication that the poet was not altogether unacceptable in polite society.

A distinctive feature of Hebrew poetry much emphasized by Lowth is its antiphonal or responsive character. Much of it was designed to be spoken or chanted by two groups; as Lowth has it, "One of the choirs sung a single verse to the other, while the other constantly added a verse in some respect correspondent to the former." In addition to numerous examples of Biblical poetry so written, he cites passages in the Bible directly referring to the practice, such as 1 Samuel 18.7 and Isaiah 6.3.

These principles form the basis for Smart's experiment. Moreover, he had been giving serious thought to a reformation of the Anglican liturgy. Many portions of the service in the Book of Common Prayer of the Church of England display these same characteristics, and readings from the Psalter are commonly performed responsively. When he later published his metrical paraphrase of the Psalms it was with the avowed intention of effecting such a reform; his version was to replace the Prayer Book version. In the same volume, it will be recalled, he published his cycle of hymns for the church year, and reprinted *A Song to David*, as if he hoped that it too might somehow be incorporated into the service. Since the *Song* is the immediate descendant of *Jubilate Agno*, it is more than probable that *Jubilate* was initially conceived as the opening move in this campaign of reform. That would explain why Smart found the principles outlined by Lowth peculiarly appropriate for his purposes. It is why the title and peroration of *Jubilate Agno* are so closely parallel to portions of the Order for Morning Prayer and the Psalter. The poem was intended as a responsive reading; and that is why the *Let* and *For* sections are physically distinct while corresponding verse for verse. Very few of the *Let* verses, until we come to Section D, contain references personal to Smart; these are nearly all confined to the *For* verses. If, then, he visualized an actual performance of *Jubilate Agno*, it was apparently with himself as the second reader or responder.

INTRODUCTION

The composition of *Jubilate Agno* extended over a period of some four years,[1] and during that time its plan and purpose underwent constant change. Of course it is impossible to say how much of this change was due to Smart's varying mental health, how much to conscious modification of method, and how much to the tedium of confinement and other intangible factors. But when Smart began *Jubilate Agno* he can hardly have intended such a lengthy piece as it eventually became. The dates afford some evidence of his shifting attitude: in the early portions they indicate an irregular flow of composition, while towards the end he was grinding out one line (or one pair of lines) per day with monotonous regularity. Between these extremes, varying rates of composition may be observed, and taken all together they show that *Jubilate Agno* began as a genuine outpouring of poetical inspiration and ended as a device with little purpose beyond recording the passage of time, as mechanical as the notches on Crusoe's stick. Any intention of printing or public performance must have vanished long before Smart reached the end.

It is a great misfortune that the responses to the opening *Let* verses have not survived. Without doubt Smart's scheme of composition was to be seen there to best advantage. The *Let* verses of Fragment A, particularly near the beginning, are the most artfully composed of any in the poem and show a structural variety not to be found in the later verses. There is also some attempt to associate the Biblical personages with appropriate animals—an attempt foredoomed to failure by the sheer scarcity of animals in the Bible, but nevertheless evidence of logical plan. One suspects that if this opening portion had survived intact its tone and content would be found to resemble in many ways those of parts of the Anglican service, and that the missing *For* verses might lack the strong personal reference which characterizes many of the surviving ones later in the poem. At any rate, the personal note is not sounded at all in Fragment A.

Fragment B1 is the earliest part in which we can watch the interplay of thought between the *Let* and *For* sections, and it is important to remember that one pair of double folios once intervened between it and Fragment A, which may thus have been begun six months or even a year earlier than Fragment B1. To use it as a basis for speculation about the missing *For* verses of Fragment A would be dangerous. But in general the *Let* verses preserve the impersonality of those in Fragment A, while the *For* verses repeatedly apply their ideas to Smart's immediate personal situation. His confinement; his past history; his future prospects; and above all, his family

[1] There are no dates in Fragment A; the earliest date in Fragment B1 is 13 August [1759], and the last line of Fragment D was probably written on 30 January 1763. My own belief is that *Jubilate Agno* is entirely the product of Smart's last confinement for insanity, and that none of it dates from the year spent in St. Luke's Hospital, 1757–1758.

21

troubles—all are related to the rather impersonal statements of the *Let* verses, which thereby take on new significance.

What emerges most forcibly is Smart's great bitterness towards his family, which is evident throughout but which .reaches a climax in the passage beginning with line 46. This passage also illustrates how both halves of the composition gain in meaning and strength by being placed together. The *Let* verses taken alone do not appear to differ in tone from others around them; the *For* verses give the impression that Smart entertained towards his mother only the kindliest of feelings. Put them together, and symbols of cuckoldry, stupidity, and greed are suddenly combined with Smart's renunciation of his birthright. It becomes transparently evident that Smart felt he had been jobbed into the asylum and done out of his rights, and thus light is shed on a vexed point in his biography. No wonder Smart would have nothing to do with his family when he was free once more, and studiously disregarded the subject of a reconciliation when it was proposed by the well-meaning Hawkesworth. The breach was far too deep to heal.

It is impossible to say where this pattern of personal reference began, if indeed it did not start with the opening of the poem; but its decline and termination may be observed midway through Fragment B1. As early as verses 19–21 the two halves divide, each going its own way momentarily, and then rejoin. At about line 155 they diverge quite widely and thereafter coincide only occasionally. The *Let* verses continue their impersonal course; the *For* verses become the vehicle for more or less coherent speculations on theological and scientific themes. Section B2, which consists of the *For* verses only of the next two double folios, is in precisely the same manner, and we may safely guess that the corresponding *Let* verses had only occasional and tenuous links with them. It is to be doubted whether the missing *Let* verses would have anything to do with the celebrated passage on Smart's cat Jeoffry (lines 697–770) which ends the fragment. In connection with this passage it is also worth remembering that its ending is not contrived, but merely the accidental result of the loss of part of the manuscript.

The 162 pairs of *Let* and *For* verses which make up Fragment C confirm this hypothesis about the disintegration of Smart's original plan. Their physical agreement is perfect; their dates show that they were written concurrently; and they are almost totally independent as to content. They lie midway between Fragment B1 and the end of the poem, and they show that the breakdown of the antiphonal scheme, which began so markedly about the middle of Fragment B1, continued until it was virtually complete at this point. The *Let* verses taken by themselves reflect this general deterioration. Their formula, with a few exceptions, has become completely mechanical; the Biblical names are drawn from a few passages only, and with no attempt to distinguish between place-names and personal names (only persons had been invoked in earlier fragments); no greater thought has been bestowed on the plant-names with which they are linked. And the personal note intrudes more often than hitherto; for example, in such lines as 68–70 and 74, in which certain herbs remind Smart of his own pulmonary ailments, or 122, where he commemorates his fortieth birthday. The *For* verses exhibit considerably more variety, but even they begin with a fragment of Smart's third and most ridiculous exercise on the alphabet, and go on to include some of his most fantastic and least intelligible speculations. His attitude towards the poem had altered entirely. Either he had lost sight of the original functions of the *Let* and *For* verses, or he chose deliberately to disregard them. This may well be a sign of renewed mental disturbance, especially since no normal man would continue such a dual poem long after its duality had ceased to serve any useful purpose. But the surrounding circumstances were far from normal. He chafed at a confinement which was certainly involuntary, and possibly he may be excused for turning a conscious work of literature into a mere device to mark the passage of time, a checking off of days on the calendar before his hoped-for release.

By Fragment D the deterioration is complete. Its earliest line shows the senseless pattern into which the verse has fallen: "Let Dew, house of Dew rejoice with Xanthenes a precious stone of an amber colour." The personal names are not Biblical and their selection is almost completely unsystematic. The names of natural objects are likewise chosen almost at random, and a series all in one category will be rudely broken into by irrelevant references to objects of a totally different sort.

It is possible that no *For* verses were ever written to accompany these *Let* verses. Certainly there is a greater intrusion into them of those personal elements mainly found in the earlier *For* verses. But still these intrusions are not frequent enough, and they do not completely satisfy the functions of the *For* verses. My own belief, impossible of proof short of recovering the missing fragments, is that Smart adhered to his basic scheme to the very end.

He composed this final section at the steady rate of one line (or, if my guess is correct, one pair of lines) per day. In the antepenultimate line he invokes a blessing on John Sherrat, the man whom he later credited with a major part in obtaining his release. The last line was written, it may be calculated, on or about 30 January 1763, and the ending of *Jubilate Agno* may be taken with a high degree of probability to coincide with the beginning of Smart's freedom.

The structure of *Jubilate Agno* and the history of its changes of plan are only half of its puzzle and fascination. At least as important and interesting is the problem of the sources of the enormous variety of material that went into it. That is a large subject, too large to treat here. The introduction, notes, and appendices to Mr. Stead's edition reveal its complexities, and such notes as I have been able to add may carry the study a little farther, but much

INTRODUCTION

remains to be done. It is clear, for example, that Smart was drawing on his entire past experience, his personal life, and his reading; point after point is illuminated by reference to his biography or to the books he presumably knew. But how much of this was memory, and how much direct reference to books? The evidence is contradictory. When we find him using a New Testament spelling in a series of names from the Old Testament, that is surely faulty memory; but when on the other hand he uses a spelling-variant peculiar to a specific passage, surrounded by other names from the same passage, we suspect that the book was open before him. And what are we to make of the alphabetical sequences of natural objects? Is it possible that his mind worked in such an orderly manner, or was he using some book with alphabetical arrangement in contents or index? If the latter, the puzzle is not at an end; for no book has yet been found containing any of these sequences. That is not to say that no such book exists.

A further problem that can only be touched on here and in the notes is that of the limits of Smart's knowledge and the sources of his thought. How much is original with him and how much derivative? For example, how much Hebrew did he know? Puns and echoes of sound and meaning run through *Jubilate Agno*, but hardly ever do they appear to depend on an understanding of Hebrew. Some of the Biblical names are actually the names of animals, but not once does Smart couple such a name with the appropriate beast. We do not expect him to miss such opportunities, and suspicion of the extent of his Hebrew grows thereby. Again, how much of his rather fantastic philosophical and scientific speculations were his own, and how much borrowed from his credulous contemporaries and predecessors? Here a different impression is received, for research has provided authorities for many of the wildest of Smart's flights, with the result that the burden of proof now rests with those who would claim that a given passage represents pure fancy or the ravings of a madman. Much also remains to be done in the attempt to identify the precise sources of Smart's information. We know that much of his natural history is taken from Pliny; Smart himself tells us so; yet the editions of Pliny which he knew and used still elude us. A glance at Mr. Stead's "Appendix II. Smart's Latin Words" will show the difficulties involved.

All of these avenues of exploration and speculation would be of no more value than a parlour-game if in the end they only returned to *Jubilate Agno* itself. But this strange poem, compounded of wisdom and madness and innocence, arid wastes and flashes of startling beauty, is not an object to be studied in isolation. It provides the entrée into the amazing, crowded lumber-room of Christopher Smart's mind at the moment when that mind was in crisis. It must be of the greatest interest and importance not only to those examining its author's development as a poet, but to all inquirers into the nature of the poetic process.

THE TEXT AND ITS ANNOTATION

THIS text represents an entirely new reading and an entirely new arrangement of the holograph manuscript, in which the intention is to give the poem as nearly as possible as its author left it. Smart made several important deletions, and I reproduce in the textual notes as much of these as can be read. He made a few revisions and corrections, and these are followed, with the uncorrected form preserved in the textual notes. He failed to correct many more slips of the pen, misspellings, and the like; these, silently corrected in the text, are also recorded in the textual notes. My aim has been to present the poem fairly and accurately while playing down such accidentals as might falsely intensify its eccentricity. Any reader curious to restore these elements in the manuscript can readily do so with the aid of the textual apparatus. The physical arrangement of the present text has already been explained at length.

The only other full edition based directly on the manuscript is *Rejoice in the Lamb*, edited by William Force Stead (1939). My textual notes also record the points at which my reading disagrees with his. All other texts (except the selections in Auden and Pearson's *Poets of the English Language*, noted above) derive from Stead's, and it does not seem worth while to record such further variants as they may accidentally provide.

Mr. Stead with unexampled generosity gave me full permission to make whatever use I chose of his explanatory annotation. His work is indispensable, and will remain so to anyone delving deeply into the complexities of the poem. He tracked down hundreds of obscure references, and proved thereby that many of the most fantastic statements in *Jubilate Agno* were not the fabrications of a lunatic but reflected wide reading and commonly accepted "fact." That fallacy is scotched, and now anyone who claims that a given passage shows madness must prove it. On the other hand, many of Smart's citations of Biblical personages and natural objects are without immediate significance, and their precise reference or definition does not assist in the understanding and appreciation of the poem. I have therefore generally avoided annotation which merely gives a possible source for some particular fact, name, or opinion, and have limited myself almost entirely to notes designed to shed light directly on the poem itself, with particular emphasis on notes deriving from or pertaining to Smart's other writings.

ACKNOWLEDGEMENTS

THOSE who may examine the introduction and notes to this edition will be constantly aware of my great indebtedness to the first editor of *Jubilate Agno*, Mr. William Force Stead. He has permitted me to make free and unrestricted use of the apparatus he so painstakingly compiled. I have also had several long and stimulating letters from a more recent editor of Smart, Mr. Robert Brittain, particularly on the subject of the time-scheme of the poem's composition. And if there is any merit in the presentation of this material, credit is certainly due to Mr. G. W. Cottrell, Jr., whose skilful editorial labours saw through the press my first article on this subject in the *Harvard Library Bulletin*. Most helpful advice and encouragement came from Professors W. A. Jackson and George Sherburn, while the dedication of this book records a kindly influence I feel in every scholarly task I undertake. During the tenure of a Fulbright Research Fellowship, the hospitality of the Department of Manuscripts of the British Museum provided me with an ideal place in which to put the finishing touches to my work.

Finally, for making the holograph manuscript of *Jubilate Agno* available to me for examination and study, I have to thank the Friends of the Harvard College Library, whose funds made possible its acquisition. In thanking them I join the growing numbers of present-day students, and link hands with the numerous company of those of the future, who owe to their generosity the collection and preservation of human knowledge in the treasures of the past.

W. H. B.

ABBREVIATIONS

THE letter *S* following a note or part of a note means that it is based upon the annotation in William Force Stead's edition. Notes or parts of notes without it are my own.

In Biblical references the abbreviations used in James Hastings's *Dictionary of the Bible* have been employed. The following additional abbreviations and short forms of reference have been used:

Albin: Eleazar Albin, *A Natural History of Birds*, 3 vol. (London, 1731–1738).
Anson: George Anson, *A Voyage round the World*, compiled by Richard Walter (London, 1748).
Brittain: *Poems by Christopher Smart*, ed. Robert Brittain (Princeton, 1950).
Callan: *The Collected Poems of Christopher Smart*, ed. Norman Callan, 2 vol. (London and Cambridge, Mass., 1949).
D.N.B.: *Dictionary of National Biography*.
N.E.D.: *New English Dictionary*.
N.T.: New Testament.
O.T.: Old Testament.
S.D.: *A Song to David*.

FRAGMENT A

ONLY the *Let* verses of the beginning of *Jubilate Agno* survive—113 lines occupying the four pages of a double folio numbered "1" by Smart. They are here printed continuously, although there can be little doubt that he also composed *For* verses to go with them. No dates occur in the text of Fragment A.

Jubilate Agno.[1]

1. Rejoice in God, O ye Tongues; give the glory to the Lord, and the Lamb.

Nations, and languages, and every Creature, in which is the breath of Life.

Let man and beast appear before him, and magnify his name together.

Let Noah and his company approach the throne of Grace, and do homage to the Ark of their Salvation.

5 Let Abraham present a Ram, and worship the God of his Redemption.[2]

Let Isaac, the Bridegroom, kneel with his Camels, and bless the hope of his pilgrimage.

Let Jacob, and his speckled Drove adore the good Shepherd of Israel.

Let Esau offer a scape Goat for his seed, and rejoice in the blessing of God his father.

Let Nimrod, the mighty hunter, bind a Leopard to the altar, and consecrate his spear to the Lord.

10 Let Ishmael dedicate a Tyger,[3] and give praise for the liberty, in which the Lord has let him at large.

Let Balaam appear with an Ass, and bless the Lord his people and his creatures for a reward eternal.

---

[1] The title of the poem is suggested by those of Ps. 66 and 100 in the Psalter of the Book of Common Prayer; the peroration is suggested by the liturgy and also owes something to Rev.7.9–10.

"After this I beheld, and, lo, a great multitude, which no man could number, of all nations, and kindreds, and people, and tongues, stood before the throne, and before the Lamb, clothed with white robes, and palms in their hands;

"And cried with a loud voice, saying, Salvation to our God which sitteth upon the throne, and unto the Lamb."

[2] Stead points out the methodical association of man and creature which begins here and continues through the first forty or fifty lines. But the roll of Biblical flora and fauna is not large, and Smart soon runs out of appropriate pairs. Many of the animals in these early lines also appear in *S.D.*; see especially lines 17 and 20 below.

[3] The *tiger* is the first non-Biblical beast to appear.

FRAGMENT A

Let Anah, the son of Zibion, lead a Mule to the temple, and bless God, who amerces the consolation of the creature for the service of Man.

Let Daniel come forth with a Lion, and praise God with all his might through faith in Christ Jesus.

Let Naphtali with an Hind give glory in the goodly words of Thanksgiving.

15 Let Aaron, the high priest, sanctify a Bull, and let him go free to the Lord and Giver of Life.

Let the Levites of the Lord take the Beavers of yᵉ brook alive into the Ark of the Testimony.[1]

Let Eleazar with the Ermine [2] serve the Lord decently and in purity.

Let Ithamar minister with a Chamois, and bless the name of Him, which cloatheth the naked.

Let Gershom with an Pygarg [3] bless the name of Him, who feedeth the hungry.

20 Let Merari praise the wisdom and power of God with the Coney, who scoopeth the rock, and archeth in the sand.[4]

Let Kohath serve with the Sable, and bless God in the ornaments of the Temple.

Let Jehoiada bless God with an Hare, whose mazes are determined for the health of the body and to parry the adversary.[5]

Let Ahitub humble himself with an Ape before Almighty God, who is the maker of variety and pleasantry.

Let Abiathar with a Fox praise the name of the Lord, who ballances craft against strength and skill against number.

---

[1] The *beaver* is non-Biblical, and as Stead points out, the usage of *Ark* in this line represents a confusion of ideas.

[2] "And ermine, jealous of a speck
    With fear eludes offence." *S.D.*, 368–369.

[3] In the MS., *Hart.* is written in Smart's hand between the lines above *Pygarg* and in a different ink. It must be an alternative, as the words are not equivalent; the pygarg is a bison appearing in Dt.14.5. This is the only example of a possible alternative reading in the entire MS.

[4] "Her cave the mining coney scoops." *S.D.*, 148.

[5] *The adversary* is not only the hare's pursuer but also Satan, a connotation frequent in this poem.

25 Let Moses, the Man of God, bless with a Lizard, in the sweet majesty of good-nature, and the magnanimity of meekness.

Let Joshua praise God with an Unicorn—the swiftness of the Lord, and the strength of the Lord, and the spear of the Lord mighty in battle.

Let Caleb with an Ounce praise the Lord of the Land of beauty and rejoice in the blessing of his good Report.

Let Othniel praise God with the Rhinoceros, who put on his armour for the reward of beauty in the Lord.

Let Tola bless with the Toad, which is the good creature of God, tho' his virtue is in the secret, and his mention is not made.[1]

30 Let Barak praise with the Pard—and great is the might of the faithful and great is the Lord in the nail of Jael and in the sword of the Son of Abinoam.[2]

Let Gideon bless with the Panther—the Word of the Lord is invincible by him that lappeth from the brook.[3]

Let Jotham praise with the Urchin, who took up his parable and provided himself for the adversary to kick against the pricks.[4]

Let Boaz, the Builder of Judah, bless with the Rat, which dwelleth in hardship and peril, that they may look to themselves and keep their houses in order.[5]

Let Obed-Edom with a Dormouse praise the Name of the Lord God his Guest for increase of his store and for peace.[6]

35 Let Abishai bless with the Hyæna—the terror of the Lord, and the fierceness of his wrath against the foes of the King and of Israel.

Let Ethan praise with the Flea, his coat of mail, his piercer, and his

---

[1] *And his mention is not made, i.e.,* in the Bible; showing that Smart was fully aware that some of his creatures were Biblical, some were not.

[2] *Barak* was the son of Abinoam and fought against Sisera, whom Jael slew with a nail (Jg.4)—a theme recurring in B1.4.

[3] *Gideon* was assisted by those who "lapped" water from the brook (Jg.7.4–7). *S.*

[4] The bramble of *Jotham's parable* (Jg.9.7 ff.) recalls the urchin or hedgehog; "to kick against the pricks" comes from Ac.9.5 and 26.14.

[5] *Boaz* became the husband of Ruth; not Boaz but Ruth is bidden to be like the "two [who] did build the house of Israel" (Ruth 4.11). *S.*

[6] *Obed-Edom* was entrusted with the Ark by David (2 S.6.10); it brought a blessing to the house and was thus (in Smart's phrase) both a "guest" and the source of an "increase of store." *S.*

vigour, which wisdom and providence have contrived to attract observation and to escape it.

Let Heman bless with the Spider, his warp and his woof, his subtlety and industry, which are good.

Let Chalcol praise with the Beetle,[1] whose life is precious in the sight of God, tho his appearance is against him.

Let Darda with a Leech bless the Name of the Physician of body & soul.

40 Let Mahol praise the Maker of Earth and Sea with the Otter, whom God has given to dive and to burrow for his preservation.

Let David bless with the Bear—The beginning of victory to the Lord— to the Lord the perfection of excellence—Hallelujah from the heart of God, and from the hand of the artist inimitable, and from the echo of the heavenly harp in sweetness magnifical and mighty.[2]

Let Solomon praise with the Ant, and give the glory to the Fountain of all Wisdom.

Let Romamti-ezer bless with the Ferret—The Lord is a rewarder of them, that diligently seek him.

Let Samuel, the Minister from a child, without ceasing praise with the Porcupine, which is the creature of defence and stands upon his arms continually.

45 Let Nathan with the Badger bless God for his retired fame, and privacy inaccessible to slander.

Let Joseph, who from the abundance of his blessing may spare to him that lacketh, praise with the Crocodile, which is pleasant and pure, when he is interpreted, tho' his look is of terror and offence.

Let Esdras bless Christ Jesus with the Rose and his people, which is a nation of living sweetness.

Let Mephibosheth with the Cricket praise the God of cheerfulness, hospitality, and gratitude.

---

[1] The Hebrew for beetle, *chargol*, may have been suggested by the name *Chalcol*. If this is not merely coincidence, it is one of the very few instances in the poem of a possible association of ideas based on a knowledge of Hebrew. See also notes on B1.24, B2.477, and B2.603.

[2] The length of the reference to David and the "Hallelujah" testify to Smart's enthusiasm. David slays the bear in 1 S.17.36, an event referred to in *S.D.*, 77–78. *S.*

Let Shallum with the Frog bless God for the meadows of Canaan, the fleece, the milk and the honey.

50 Let Hilkiah praise with the Weasel, which sneaks for his prey in craft, and dwelleth at ambush.

Let Job bless with the Worm—the life of the Lord is in Humiliation, the Spirit also and the truth.

Let Elihu bless with the Tortoise, which is food for praise and thanksgiving.[1]

Let Hezekiah praise with the Dromedary—the zeal for the glory of God is excellence, and to bear his burden is grace.

Let Zadok worship with the Mole—before honour is humility, and he that looketh low shall learn.

55 Let Gad [2] with the Adder bless in the simplicity of the preacher and the wisdom of the creature.

Let Tobias bless Charity with his Dog, who is faithful, vigilant, and a friend in poverty.[3]

Let Anna bless God with the Cat, who is worthy to be presented before the throne of grace, when he has trampled upon the idol in his prank.[4]

Let Benaiah praise with the Asp—to conquer malice is nobler, than to slay the lion.[5]

Let Barzillai bless with Snail—a friend in need is as the balm of Gilead, or as the slime to the wounded bark.[6]

60 Let Joab with the Horse worship the Lord God of Hosts.[7]

---

[1] The *tortoise* as "food for praise and thanksgiving" is difficult to explain, as it is one of the unclean beasts in Lv.11.29. S.

[2] *Gad* reappears in B2.610.

[3] *Tobias*, hero of the apocryphal Book of Tobit, was accompanied by a faithful dog. S.

[4] Smart was probably thinking of the *Anna* who was Tobias's mother. The antics of the cat (which is non-Biblical) foreshadow the lines on Smart's cat Jeoffry, B2.696–770.

[5] *Benaiah* "slew a lion in the midst of a pit in time of snow," 2 S.23.20.

[6] *Barzillai* was a Gileadite (hence the reference to *Balm*) who helped David in his flight from Absalom, 2 S.17 and 19.

[7] *Joab* became one of the "captains of the host" to David, 2 S.18.2. S.

FRAGMENT A

Let Shemaiah bless God with the Caterpillar—the minister of vengeance is the harbinger of mercy.[1]

Let Ahimelech with the Locust bless God from the tyranny of numbers.

Let Cornelius with the Swine bless God, which purifyeth all things for the poor.[2]

Let Araunah bless with the Squirrel, which is a gift of homage from the poor man to the wealthy and increaseth good will.

65 Let Bakbakkar bless with the Salamander, which feedeth upon ashes as bread, and whose joy is at the mouth of the furnace.

Let Jabez bless with Tarantula, who maketh his bed in the moss, which he feedeth, that the pilgrim may take heed to his way.

Let Jakim with the Satyr bless God in the dance.—[3]

Let Iddo praise the Lord with the Moth—the writings of man perish as the garment, but the Book of God endureth for ever.

Let Nebuchadnezzar bless with the Grashopper [4]—the pomp and vanities of the world are as the herb of the field, but the glory of the Lord increaseth for ever.

70 Let Naboth bless with the Canker-worm—envy is cruel and killeth & preyeth upon that which God has given to aspire and bear fruit.[5]

Let Lud bless with the Elk, the strenuous asserter of his liberty, and the maintainer of his ground.

Let Obadiah with the Palmer-worm bless God for the remnant that is left.[6]

---

[1] Along with various worms (see A72), the *caterpillar* appears in the Bible as a symbol of destruction, the vengeance of the Lord.

[2] Smart suddenly interjects *Cornelius* from the N.T. into his catalogue of O.T. personages. Cornelius is associated with Peter's vision of God's cleansing of "all manner of fourfooted beasts of the earth, and wild beasts, and creeping things, and fowls of the air," Ac.10.12 ff.

[3] ". . . And satyrs shall dance there," Is.13.21.

[4] *Grashopper* (with one *s*) is Smart's habitual spelling, occurring also at B1.100 and D153, and it has therefore been retained. Among other appearances in the Bible, the grasshopper and Nebuchadnezzar appear in close juxtaposition in Jer.46.23 and 26.

[5] *Naboth's* death resulted from Ahab's envy of his vineyard, 1 K.21. S.

[6] The book of *Obadiah* concerns the scattering and destruction of the Edomites; and in its two appearances in the Bible the *palmer-worm* is used as the symbol of such destruction (Joel 1.4, Amos 4.9).

Let Agur bless with the Cockatrice—The consolation of the world is deceitful, and temporal honour the crown of him that creepeth.

Let Ithiel bless with the Baboon, whose motions are regular in the wilderness, and who defendeth himself with a staff against the assailant.[1]

75 Let Ucal bless with the Cameleon, which feedeth on the Flowers and washeth himself in the dew.

Let Lemuel bless with the Wolf, which is a dog without a master, but the Lord hears his cries and feeds him in the desert.

Let Hananiah bless with the Civet, which is pure from benevolence.

Let Azariah bless with the Reindeer, who runneth upon the waters, and wadeth thro the land in snow.

Let Mishael bless with the Stoat—the praise of the Lord gives propriety to all things.

80 Let Savaran [2] bless with the Elephant, who gave his life for his country that he might put on immortality.

Let Nehemiah, the imitator of God, bless with the Monkey, who is workd down from Man.[3]

Let Manasses [4] bless with the Wild-Ass—liberty begetteth insolence, but necessity is the mother of prayer.

Let Jebus bless with the Camelopard, which is good to carry and to parry and to kneel.

Let Huz bless with the Polypus—lively subtlety is acceptable to the Lord.

85 Let Buz bless with the Jackall—but the Lord is the Lion's provider.

Let Meshullam bless with the Dragon, who maketh his den in desolation and rejoiceth amongst the ruins.[5]

---

[1] The *baboon* defending himself with a staff is frequent in eighteenth-century natural history. *S*.

[2] *Savaran* is not a Biblical name, nor does it appear to be a distortion of one. I can find no good explanation for its intrusion.

[3] *Nehemiah* rebuilt the ruined Jerusalem. The monkey "who is workd down from man" is a contrast to Nehemiah, "the imitator of God." Buffon has a chapter on the "Degeneration of Animals." *S*.

[4] *Manasses* is the N.T. spelling of the O.T. Manasseh.

[5] The *dragon* amid ruins and desolation appears in Jer.9.11 and 10.22.

FRAGMENT A

Let Enoch bless with the Rackoon, who walked with God as by the instinct.[1]

Let Hashbadana bless with the Catamountain, who stood by the Pulpit of God against the dissensions of the Heathen.[2]

Let Ebed-Melech bless with the Mantiger, the blood of the Lord is sufficient to do away the offence of Cain, and reinstate the creature which is amerced.

90 Let A Little Child [3] with a Serpent bless Him, who ordaineth strength in babes to the confusion of the Adversary.

Let Huldah [4] bless with the Silkworm—the ornaments of the Proud are from the bowells of their Betters.

Let Susanna bless with the Butterfly—beauty hath wings, but chastity is the Cherub.

Let Sampson bless with the Bee,[5] to whom the Lord hath given strength to annoy the assailant and wisdom to his strength.

Let Amasiah bless with the Chaffer—the top of the tree is for the brow of the champion, who has given the glory to God.

95 Let Hashum [6] bless with the Fly, whose health is the honey of the air, but he feeds upon the thing strangled, and perisheth.

Let Malchiah bless with the Gnat—it is good for man and beast to mend their pace.

Let Pedaiah bless with the Humble-Bee, who loves himself in solitude and makes his honey alone.

Let Maaseiah bless with the Drone, who with the appearance of a Bee is neither a soldier nor an artist, neither a swordsman nor smith.

---

[1] "And Enoch walked with God," Gn.5.22.

[2] *Hashbadana* stood with Ezra when he read the Law to the people, Neh.8.4.

[3] "A Little Child" (Is.11.6) illustrates the startling naïveté of some of Smart's references.

[4] *Huldah* means *weasel*: one of Smart's lost opportunities for a bilingual association.

[5] ". . . Thy type
   The lion and the bee." *S.D.*, 227–228.
Samson found a swarm of bees and honey in the carcase of a lion (Jg.14.8).

[6] *Hashum* and the next five names were probably taken by Smart from Neh.8.4. This is the earliest instance in the poem of Smart's habit of using in a group a series of names from a given Biblical passage.

Let Urijah bless with the Scorpion, which is a scourge against the murmurers—the Lord keep it from our coasts.

100 Let Anaiah bless with the Dragon-fly, who sails over the pond by the wood-side and feedeth on the cressies.

Let Zorobabel [1] bless with the Wasp, who is the Lord's architect, and buildeth his edifice in armour.

Let Jehu bless with the Hornet, who is the soldier of the Lord to extirpate abomination and to prepare the way of peace. [2]

Let Mattithiah bless with the Bat, who inhabiteth the desolations of pride and flieth amongst the tombs.

Let Elias [3] which is the innocency of the Lord rejoice with the Dove.

105 Let Asaph rejoice with the Nightingale—The musician of the Lord! and the watchman of the Lord! [4]

Let Shema rejoice with the Glowworm, who is the lamp of the traveller and mead of the musician.

Let Jeduthun rejoice with the Woodlark, who is sweet and various.

Let Chenaniah rejoice with Chloris, [5] in the vivacity of his powers and the beauty of his person.

Let Gideoni rejoice with the Goldfinch, who is shrill and loud, and full withal.

110 Let Giddalti rejoice with the Mocking-bird, who takes off the notes of the Aviary and reserves his own.

Let Jogli rejoice with the Linnet, who is distinct and of mild delight.

Let Benjamin bless and rejoice with the Redbird, who is soft and soothing.

Let Dan rejoice with the Blackbird, who praises God with all his heart, and biddeth to be of good cheer.

---

[1] *Zorobabel* is the N.T. spelling of O.T. Zerubabel.

[2] *Jehu* was the general of the Israelites who was called to "extirpate the abomination" of Baal-worship (2 K.9 and 10). *S.*

[3] *Elias* is the N.T. spelling of O.T. Elijah.

[4] In 1 Ch.6.39 *Asaph* is among those "whom David set over the service of song in the house of the Lord." *S.*

[5] *Chloris*, the Indian green finch, was to be seen in London, as attested by George Edwards, *A Natural History of Uncommon Birds* (1743), I, 84 and 127. *S.*

FRAGMENT B1

THE next surviving fragment was numbered "3" by Smart at the head of both the *Let* and the *For* verses, each of which sections comprises 295 lines written on four pages of a double folio. Clearly there once intervened between Fragments A and B1 another pair of double folios, one each of *Let* and *For* verses, each numbered "2". At this point, then, there is a lacuna of undeterminable length—presumably of something between 110 and 300 pairs of antiphonal lines. Dates in Fragment B1 place its composition in the autumn of 1759.

Both the *Let* and the *For* verses of Fragment B1 survive, and they are printed here *vis-à-vis*, so that the identity of each portion is preserved while its relationship to the other is plainly revealed.

JUBILATE AGNO

3. Let Elizur rejoice with the Partridge,[1] who is a prisoner of state and is proud of his keepers.

Let Shedeur rejoice with Pyrausta,[2] who dwelleth in a medium of fire, which God hath adapted for him.

Let Shelumiel rejoice with Olor,[3] who is of a goodly savour, and the very look of him harmonizes the mind.

Let Jael rejoice with the Plover, who whistles for his live, and foils the marksmen and their guns.[4]

5 Let Raguel rejoice with the Cock of Portugal—God send good Angels to the allies of England![5]

Let Hobab rejoice with Necydalus, who is the Greek of a Grub.

Let Zurishaddai with the Polish Cock rejoice—The Lord restore peace to Europe.

Let Zuar rejoice with the Guinea Hen—The Lord add to his mercies in the WEST!

Let Chesed rejoice with Strepsiceros,[6] whose weapons are the ornaments of his peace.

10 Let Hagar rejoice with Gnesion, who is the right sort of eagle, and towers the highest.

Let Libni rejoice with the Redshank, who migrates not but is translated to the upper regions.[7]

Let Nahshon rejoice with the Seabreese, the Lord give the sailors of his Spirit.

Let Helon rejoice with the Woodpecker—the Lord encourage the propagation of trees!

---

[1] A caged quail figures in Smart's fable, "The English Bull Dog, Dutch Mastiff, and Quail," Callan, I, 59.

[2] *Pyrausta*, a winged insect said to dwell in the fire. *S.*

[3] *Olor*, swan. *S.* Smart connects this with *olere*, to savour of or to smell of.

[4] *Jael* has already appeared in A30. *Live* is an archaic spelling of *life*.

[5] About this time the Portuguese were threatened by Spain for refusing to join her against Great Britain. *S.*

[6] *Strepsiceros*, a sheep or goat with twisted horns. *S.*

[7] Such notions of bird migration were not at all uncommon in Smart's day. *S.*

FRAGMENT B1

3. For I am not without authority in my jeopardy, which I derive inevitably from the glory of the name of the Lord.

For I bless God whose name is Jealous—and there is a zeal to deliver us from everlasting burnings.

For my existimation [1] is good even amongst the slanderers and my memory shall arise for a sweet savour unto the Lord.

For I bless the PRINCE of PEACE and pray that all the guns may be nail'd up, save such as are for the rejoicing days.

5 For I have abstained from the blood of the grape and that even at the Lord's table.

For I have glorified God in GREEK and LATIN, the consecrated languages spoken by the Lord on earth. [2]

For I meditate the peace of Europe amongst family bickerings and domestic jars. [3]

For the HOST is in the WEST—the Lord make us thankful unto salvation.

For I preach the very GOSPEL of CHRIST without comment & with this weapon shall I slay envy.

10 For I bless God in the rising generation, which is on my side.

For I have translated in the charity, which makes things better & I shall be translated myself at the last.

For he that walked upon the sea, hath prepared the floods with the Gospel of peace.

For the merciful man is merciful to his beast, and to the trees that give them shelter.

---

[1] *N.E.D.* does not record *existimation*, but rather than an error for "estimation" the word appears to be a coinage from *existimare* and the phrase *my existimation* to mean "my reputation" or "the esteem in which I am held."

[2] Greek and Latin as consecrated languages recur in B2.647.

[3] This presumably refers to the Seven Years War (1756–1763) which coincided almost exactly with the period of Smart's confinement. *S.*

JUBILATE AGNO

Let Amos rejoice with the Coote—prepare to meet thy God, O Israel.

15 Let Ephah rejoice with Buprestis,[1] the Lord endue us with temperance & humanity, till every cow have her mate!

Let Sarah rejoice with the Redwing,[2] whose harvest is in the frost and snow.

Let Rebekah rejoice with Iynx,[3] who holds his head on one side to deceive the adversary.

Let Shuah rejoice with Boa, which is the vocal serpent.

Let Ehud rejoice with Onocrotalus,[4] whose braying is for the glory of God, because he makes the best musick in his power.

20 Let Shamgar rejoice with Otis,[5] who looks about him for the glory of God, & sees the horizon compleat at once.

Let Bohan rejoice with the Scythian Stag—he is beef and breeches against want & nakedness.

Let Achsah rejoice with the Pigeon who is an antidote to malignity [6] and will carry a letter.

Let Tohu rejoice with the Grouse—the Lord further the cultivating of heaths & the peopling of deserts.

---

[1] *Buprestis*, an insect in Pliny harmful to cattle. *S.*

[2] *Redwing* is a thrush which like the fieldfare (B1.57) is seen in England only in the winter. See Albin, I, 33.

[3] *Iynx*, a bird, the wryneck, cited in William Derham's *Physico-Theology* (1713), p. 242, n. 12, as an instance of self-preservation. *S.*

[4] *Onocrotalus*, a large waterfowl, supposed to be the bittern or cormorant. *S.*

[5] *Otis*, a species of bustard. *S.* It was said to have difficulty in taking flight, and therefore to keep a sharp watch and take wing when any possible enemy was still far away; see Albin, III, 36.

[6] A fresh-killed pigeon was split and placed on a festering wound to draw out the poison.

For he hath turned the shadow of death into the morning, the Lord is his name.[1]

15 For I am come home again, but there is nobody to kill the calf or to pay the musick.

For the hour of my felicity, like the womb of Sarah, shall come at the latter end.

For I shou'd have avail'd myself of waggery, had not malice been multitudinous.

For there are still serpents that can speak—God bless my head, my heart & my heel.

For I bless God that I am of the same seed as Ehud, Mutius Scævola, and Colonel Draper.[2]

20 For the word of God is a sword on my side—no matter what other weapon a stick or a straw.[3]

For I have adventured myself in the name of the Lord, and he hath mark'd me for his own.

For I bless God for the Postmaster general & all conveyancers of letters under his care especially Allen & Shelvock.[4]

For my grounds in New Canaan shall infinitely compensate for the flats & maynes of Staindrop Moor.[5]

---

[1] Smart derives versicle and response by abridging and combining Amos 4.12 and 5.8.

[2] *Ehud* was the warrior of Jg.3.15; *Mutius Scævola* was the hero who opposed Porsena. *Col. Draper* was Sir William Draper, Smart's contemporary at Cambridge and hero of wars in the Orient. Smart addressed an ode to him in 1763 (Callan, I, 16), and Draper subscribed for forty copies of the *Psalms* (1765). *S.* That Ehud and Scævola were left-handed is possibly a mere coincidence; I have found no evidence about Draper, and Smart holds his pen in his right hand in the Pembroke College portrait.

[3] In this and the following line, the *For* verses depend one upon another, rather than upon their respective *Let* verses.

[4] *Ralph Allen* (1694–1764) instituted a system of cross-country posts, see *D.N.B.*; *George Shelvocke* was appointed Secretary to the Post Master General, 1742. *S.* Shelvocke also had an aviary containing various rare birds; see George Edwards, *Gleanings of Natural History* (1760), II, 176.

[5] *Staindrop Moor*, adjacent to Raby Castle, the seat of the Vane family, whose steward Smart's father was; *maynes*, a wide expanse. *S.*

JUBILATE AGNO

Let Hillel rejoice with Ammodytes,[1] whose colour is deceitful and he plots against the pilgrim's feet.

25 Let Eli rejoice with Leucon [2]—he is an honest fellow, which is a rarity.

Let Jemuel rejoice with Charadrius,[3] who is from the HEIGHT & the sight of him is good for the jaundice.

Let Pharaoh rejoice with Anataria,[4] whom God permits to prey upon the ducks to check their increase.

Let Lotan rejoice with Sauterelle.[5] Blessed be the name of the Lord from the Lote-tree to the Palm.

Let Dishon rejoice with the Landrail, God give his grace to the society for preserving the game.

30 Let Hushim rejoice with the King's Fisher, who is of royal beauty, tho' plebeian size.

Let Machir rejoice with Convolvulus, from him to the ring of Saturn, which is the girth of Job; to the signet of God from Job & his daughters BLESSED BE JESUS.[6]

Let Atad bless with Eleos, the nightly Memorialist $\varepsilon\lambda\varepsilon\eta\sigma\sigma\nu$ $\varkappa\nu\rho\iota\varepsilon$.[7]

Let Jamin rejoice with the Bittern blessed be the name of Jesus for Denver Sluice, Ruston, & the draining of the fens.[8]

---

[1] *Ammodytes*, an African serpent, a sand burrower. *S. Hillel* means "praised greatly," making this one of the rare occasions when Smart appears to derive the *For* verse from a play on the meaning of the Hebrew name.

[2] *Leucon*, a white heron, which in turn suggests the white raven in the *For* verse. White ravens were exhibited as curiosities, as was also "Thos. Hall, the gigantic boy" (1741–1747), who at the age of 38 months was four feet tall and had a deep voice. Smart may be referring to himself as a gazing-stock in the asylum. *S.*

[3] *Charadrius*, a yellow bird. *S.* But Albin (I, 76) identifies it as the Sea Lark, a black and white shore-bird.

[4] *Anataria*, an eagle. *S.*

[5] *Sauterelle*, grasshopper or locust. *S.*

[6] *Convolvulus* may be either bindweed, or a caterpillar. *S.* The *signet* on the right hand of God is referred to in Jer.22.24.

[7] *Eleos*, a kind of owl. '$\varepsilon\lambda\varepsilon\eta\sigma\sigma\nu$ $\varkappa\nu\rho\iota\varepsilon$, Lord have mercy. *S.*

[8] *Denver Sluice*, part of the seventeenth-century drainage system between Ely and King's Lynn; for the history of the draining of the fens, see *The Victoria History of the County of Cambridge* (1948), II, 76–83. *Ruston* is probably the Norfolk fenland manor of Smart's patron, Roger Pratt; see D105.

44

FRAGMENT B1

For the praise of God can give to a mute fish. the notes of a nightingale.

25 For I have seen the White Raven & Thomas Hall of Willingham & am myself a greater curiosity than both.

For I look up to heaven which is my prospect to escape envy by surmounting it.

For if Pharaoh had known Joseph, he woud have blessed God & me for the illumination of the people.

For I pray God to bless improvements in gardening till London be a city of palm-trees.

For I pray to give his grace to the poor of England, that Charity be not offended & that benevolence may increase.

30 For in my nature I quested for beauty, but God, God hath sent me to sea for pearls.

For there is a blessing from the STONE of Jesus which is founded upon hell to the precious jewell on the right hand of God.

For the nightly Visitor is at the window of the impenitent, while I sing a psalm of my own composing.

For there is a note added to the scale, which the Lord hath made fuller, stronger & more glorious.

JUBILATE AGNO

Let Ohad rejoice with Byturos [1] who eateth the vine and is a minister of temperance.

35 Let Zohar rejoice with Cychramus [2] who cometh with the quails on a particular affair.

Let Serah, the daughter of Asher, rejoice with Ceyx,[3] who maketh his cabin in the Halcyon's hold.

Let Magdiel rejoice with Ascarides,[4] which is the life of the bowels—the worm hath a part in our frame.

Let Becher rejoice with Oscen [5] who terrifies the wicked, as trumpet and alarm the coward.

Let Shaul rejoice with Circos,[6] who hath clumsy legs, but he can wheel it the better with his wings.

40 Let Hamul rejoice with the Crystal, who is pure and translucent.

Let Ziphion rejoice with the Tit-Lark who is a groundling, but he raises the spirits.

Let Mibzar rejoice with the Cadess,[7] as is their number, so are their names, blessed be the Lord Jesus for them all.

Let Jubal rejoice with Cæcilia,[8] the woman and the slow-worm praise the name of the Lord.

Let Arodi rejoice with the Royston Crow, there is a society of them at Trumpington & Cambridge.[9]

---

[1] *Bittern* reminds Smart of *Byturos*, a rodent said by Cicero to eat the vines in Campania. *S.*

[2] *Cychramus*, a bird that migrates with quails. *S.*

[3] *Ceyx*, sea-gull; see the stories of Ceyx and Alcyone in Ovid and Virgil. *S.*

[4] *Ascarides*, a worm in the intestines; Smart may have found it in Derham's *Physico-Theology*, p. 419, n. 12. *S.*

[5] *Oscen*, a bird from which auguries were taken. *S.*

[6] *Circos*, a hawk. *S.*

[7] *Cadess*, caddis, the mayfly. *S.*

[8] *Cæcilia*, a lizard; the line associates Jubal, the inventor of music, with St. Cecilia its patron. *S.*

[9] *Royston Crow*, the hooded crow; there was a colony of them at Cambridge. *S.* *Trumpington* is two miles south of Cambridge on the road to Royston.

For I offer my goat as he browses the vine, bless the Lord from chambering & drunkeness.[1]

35 For there is a traveling for the glory of God without going to Italy or France.

For I bless the children of Asher for the evil I did them & the good I might have received at their hands.

For I rejoice like a worm in the rain in him that cherishes and from him that tramples.

For I am ready for the trumpet & alarm to fight, to die & to rise again.

For the banish'd of the Lord shall come about again, for so he hath prepared for them.

40 For sincerity is a jewel which is pure & transparent, eternal & inestimable.

For my hands and my feet are perfect as the sublimity of Naphtali and the felicity of Asher.

For the names and number of animals are as the names and number of the stars.[2]

For I pray the Lord Jesus to translate my MAGNIFICAT into verse and represent it.

For I bless the Lord Jesus from the bottom of Royston Cave [3] to the top of King's Chapel.

---

[1] *Chambering and drunkeness* is a compression of the phrase in Ro.13.13.
[2] The phrase "the number of their names" occurs repeatedly in Nu.1 and 3.
[3] *Royston Cave*, a cavern under Melbourn Street, Royston. *S.*

45 Let Areli rejoice with the Criel,[1] who is a dwarf that towereth above others.

Let Phuvah rejoice with Platycerotes,[2] whose weapons of defence keep them innocent.

Let Shimron rejoice with the Kite, who is of more valuè than many sparrows.

Let Sered rejoice with the Wittal [3]—a silly bird is wise unto his own preservation.

Let Elon rejoice with Attelabus, who is the Locust without wings.

50 Let Jahleel rejoice with the Woodcock,[4] who liveth upon suction and is pure from his diet.

Let Shuni rejoice with the Gull, who is happy in not being good for food.

Let Ezbon rejoice with Musimon,[5] who is from the ram and she-goat.

Let Barkos rejoice with the Black Eagle, which is the least of his species and the best-natured.

Let Bedan [6] rejoice with Ossifrage—the bird of prey and the man of prayer.

55 Let Naomi rejoice with Pseudosphece [7] who is between a wasp and a hornet.

[1] *Criel*, the lesser white heron, or egret. *S*.

[2] *Platycerotes*, stags with broad horns. *S*. The undercurrent of bitterness in this part of the poem here rises to a climax, where in succeeding lines the Stag (horns), Kite, Wittol (cuckold), Locust, Woodcock, and Gull are associated with Smart's renunciation of his birthright. "Family bickerings and domestic jars" appeared as early as line B1.7; and the theme of cuckoldry recurs explicitly or implicitly in B1.58–59, B1.115, and elsewhere.

[3] *Wittal*, wittol, the bird whose nest is violated by the cuckoo, symbolizing the man whose wife is unfaithful.

[4] *Woodcock*, "his food is not known," Johnson's *Dictionary*. *S*.

[5] *Musimon*, probably the muflone, whence we have the tame sheep. *S*.

[6] *Bedan* was a judge of Israel, but with no particular claim to be denominated a "man of prayer."

[7] *Pseudosphece*, false or solitary wasp. *S*.

45 For I am a little fellow,[1] which is intitled to the great mess by the benevolence of God my father.

For I this day made over my inheritance to my mother in consideration of her infirmities.

For I this day made over my inheritance to my mother in consideration of her age.

For I this day made over my inheritance to my mother in consideration of her poverty.

For I bless the thirteenth of August,[2] in which I had the grace to obey the voice of Christ in my conscience.

50 For I bless the thirteenth of August, in which I was willing to run all hazards for the sake of the name of the Lord.

For I bless the thirteenth of August, in which I was willing to be called a fool for the sake of Christ.

For I lent my flocks and my herds and my lands at once unto the Lord.

For nature is more various than observation tho' observers be innumerable.

For Agricola is Γηωργος.[3]

55 For I pray God to bless POLLY in the blessing of Naomi [4] and assign her to the house of David.

---

[1] Smart was acutely conscious of his small stature; see "The Author Apologizes to a Lady for His being a Little Man," Callan, I, 112.

[2] The year-date is evidently 1759.

[3] The manuscript in this line contains three deletions which cannot be entirely read: For ⟨..........⟩ Agricola ⟨......⟩ is Γηωργος ⟨which is by the blessing of God SAINT GEORGE⟩.

[4] *Naomi's blessing* was in the child of her faithful daughter-in-law Ruth by Boaz, Obed, the grandfather of David. *Polly* is unidentified, but was mentioned by Smart as a former sweetheart in "The Lass with the Golden Locks," Callan, I, 202.

56 Let Ruth [1] rejoice with the Tumbler—it is a pleasant thing to feed him and be thankful.

Let Ram rejoice with the Fieldfare,[2] who is a good gift from God in the season of scarcity.

Let Manoah rejoice with Cerastes,[3] who is a Dragon with horns.

Let Talmai rejoice with Alcedo,[4] who makes a cradle for its young, which is rock'd by the winds.

60 Let Bukki rejoice with the Buzzard, who is clever, with the reputation of a silly fellow.

Let Michal rejoice with Leucocruta [5] who is a mixture of beauty and magnanimity.

Let Abiah rejoice with Morphnus [6] who is a bird of passage to the Heavens.

Let Hur rejoice with the Water-wag-tail, who is a neighbour, and loves to be looked at.

Let Dodo rejoice with the purple Worm, who is cloathed sumptuously, tho he fares meanly.

65 Let Ahio rejoice with the Merlin who is a cousin german of the hawk.

Let Joram rejoice with the Water Rail, who takes his delight in the river.

---

[1] *Ruth* was a Moabitess, which leads to the corresponding *For* verse. Smart elsewhere identifies the French and the Moabites; see B2.399 and 438.

[2] *Fieldfare*, a thrush wintering in England and emigrating in summer; "accounted very good meat," Francis Willughby, *Ornithology* (1678), pp. 188–189.

[3] *Cerastes*, horned serpent. *S.*

[4] *Alcedo*, a bird which breeds in the sea, the halcyon. *S.* See B1.36.

[5] *Leucocruta* (leucrocuta), a Plinean animal, with the legs of a hart and the breast of a lion. *S.*

[6] *Morphnus*, an eagle. *S.*

FRAGMENT B1

56 For I am in charity with the French who are my foes and Moabites because of the Moabitish woman.

For my Angel is always ready at a pinch to help me out and to keep me up.

For CHRISTOPHER must slay the Dragon with a PHEON's head.[1]

For they have seperated me and my bosom, whereas the right comes by setting us together.

60 For Silly fellow! Silly fellow! is against me and belongeth neither to me nor my family.

For he that scorneth the scorner hath condescended to my low estate.[2]

For Abiah is the father of Joab and Joab of all Romans and English Men.[3]

For they pass by me in their tour, and the good Samaritan is not yet come.[4]

For I bless God in the behalf of TRINITY COLLEGE in CAMBRIDGE & the society of PURPLES in LONDON.[5]

65 For I have a nephew CHRISTOPHER [6] to whom I implore the grace of God.

For I pray God bless the CAM—Mr HIGGS & Mr & Mrs WASHBOURNE as the drops of the dew.

---

[1] A deletion in this line can be read: For ⟨Agricola is SAINT GEORGE, but his son⟩ CHRISTOPHER. . . . *Pheon* in heraldry is a broad barbed arrow or the head of a dart, and it has a personal application for Smart. His family claimed descent from Sir John Smart, Garter King of Arms under Edward IV, by virtue of which Christopher Smart was entitled to bear arms: argent a chevron between three pheons sable. Christopher slaying a horned serpent or dragon may well be a return to the earlier theme of cuckoldry.

[2] Prov.3.34: "Surely he scorneth the scorners: but he giveth grace unto the lowly."

[3] Smart appears to be mistaken, as Abiah was not the father of Joab. On Joab as ancestor of the English, see B2.433.

[4] The inmates of asylums were still a public spectacle for the curious.

[5] Stead conjectures that the *Society of Purples* was an association of Cambridge men, but this has not been confirmed. The juxtaposition of lines suggests a rather pejorative overtone; it is not the only slighting reference to Cambridge—see B1.69.

[6] *Nephew Christopher*, the Rev. Christopher Hunter, who edited and wrote the introduction to Smart's *Poems* (1791). S.

67 Let Chileab rejoice with Ophion who is clean made, less than an hart, and a Sardinian.[1]

Let Shephatiah rejoice with the little Owl,[2] which is the wingged Cat.

Let Ithream rejoice with the great Owl, who understandeth that which he professes.

70 Let Abigail rejoice with Lethophagus God be gracious to the widows indeed.

Let Anathoth bless with Saurix,[3] who is a bird of melancholy.

Let Shammua rejoice with the Vultur who is strength and fierceness.

Let Shobab rejoice with Evech who is of the goat kind which is meditation and pleasantry.

Let Ittai the Gittite rejoice with the Gerfalcon amicus certus in re incertâ cernitur.

75 Let Ibhar rejoice with the Pochard a child born in prosperity is the chiefest blessing of peace.

Let Elishua rejoice with Cantharis God send bread and milk to the children.

Let Chimham rejoice with Drepanis who is a passenger from the sea to heaven.[4]

Let Toi [5] rejoice with Percnopteros which haunteth the sugar-fens.

Let Nepheg rejoice with Cenchris which is the spotted serpent.

---

[1] *Ophion*, a Plinean beast inhabiting Sardinia. At this time England was paying a subsidy to the King of Sardinia, which probably accounts for this reference and that in B2.456. S.

[2] *The little Owl* is still known to country people as the cat-owl. S.

[3] *Saurix*, a kind of owl. S.

[4] *Drepanis*, the sand martin. S. Smart's contemporaries argued as to whether this bird migrated or hibernated; see *Philosophical Transactions*, LI (1760), 463–464. *Chimham* evidently suggested a Chinese name to Smart, leading to the corresponding *For* verse.

[5] *Toi* may also have seemed like a Chinese name.

FRAGMENT B1

67 For I pray God bless the king of Sardinia and make him an instrument of his peace.

For I am possessed of a cat, surpassing in beauty, from whom I take occasion to bless Almighty God.

For I pray God for the professors of the University of Cambridge to attend & to amend.

70 For the Fatherless Children and widows are never deserted of the Lord.

For I pray God be gracious to the house of Stuart [1] and consider their afflictions.

For I pray God be gracious to the seed of Virgil to Mr GOODMAN SMITH of King's and Joseph STUD.

For I give God the glory that I am a son of ABRAHAM a PRINCE of the house of my fathers.

For my brethren have dealt deceitfully as a brook, and as the stream of brooks that pass away. [2]

75 For I bless God for my retreat at CANBURY, [3] as it was the place of the nativity of my children.

For I pray God to give them the food which I cannot earn for them any otherwise than by prayer.

For I pray God bless the Chinese which are of ABRAHAM and the Gospel grew with them at the first.

For I bless God in the honey of the sugar-cane and the milk of the cocoa.

For I bless God in the libraries of the learned & for all the booksellers in the world. [4]

---

[1] *The House of Stuart*, see also D206.
[2] A slightly inaccurate quotation of Job 6.15.
[3] *Canbury*, Canonbury House, Islington, where Smart lived after marrying. S.
[4] This pair of lines seems to reflect Smart's bitterness at some of his dealings with booksellers.

JUBILATE AGNO

80 Let Japhia rejoice with Buteo [1] who hath three testicles.

Let Gibeon rejoice with the Puttock,[2] who will shift for himself to the last extremity.

Let Elishama rejoice with Mylæcos Ισχετε χειρα μυλαιον αλιτριδες. ευδετε μακρα.[3]

Let Elimelech rejoice with the Horn-Owl who is of gravity and amongst my friends in the tower.

Let Eliada rejoice with the Gier-eagle who is swift and of great penetration.

85 Let Eliphalet rejoice with Erodius who is God's good creature, which is sufficient for him.

Let Jonathan, David's nephew, rejoice with Oripelargus who is noble by his ascent.

Let Sheva rejoice with the Hobby,[4] who is the service of the great.

Let Ahimaaz rejoice with the Silver-Worm [5] who is a living mineral.

Let Shobi rejoice with the Kastrel blessed be the name JESUS in falconry and in the MALL.

90 Let Elkanah rejoice with Cymindis [6] the Lord illuminate us against the powers of darkness.

---

[1] *Buteo*, "that sort of hawk (as Pliny witnesseth) which the Romans named Buteo, was by the Grecians called Triorches, from the number of its stones," Willughby, *Ornithology* (1678), p. 71. *S.* This myth was no longer believed by most naturalists in Smart's day; indeed, it is denounced by Willughby.

[2] *Puttock*, a buzzard equated by Willughby with Buteo. *S.*

[3] *Mylæcos*, a worm breeding in mills, whence the accompanying Greek sentence, "Stay your hand from the mill, ye grinders; long be your slumber," *Palatine Anthology*, IX, p. 418. *S.*

[4] *Hobby*, a small falcon. *S.* Perhaps it is not too fanciful to connect Hobby with Hobbes, whose controversies would bring to mind one of his opponents, Henry Hyde, first Earl of Clarendon, who appears in the matching *For* verse.

[5] *Silver-Worm*, the glow-worm. *S.*

[6] *Cymindis*, the night-hawk or nightjar. *S.*

FRAGMENT B1

80 For I bless God in the strength of my loins and for the voice which he hath made sonorous.

For tis no more a merit to provide for oneself, but to quit all for the sake of the Lord.

For there is no invention but the gift of God, and no grace like the grace of gratitude.

For grey hairs are honourable and tell every one of them to the glory of God.

For I bless the Lord Jesus for the memory of GAY, POPE and SWIFT.

85 For all good words are from GOD, and all others are cant.

For I am enobled by my ascent and the Lord haith raised me above my Peers.

For I pray God bless my lord CLARENDON and his seed for ever.

For there is silver in my mines and I bless God that it is rather there than in my coffers.

For I blessed God in St James's Park till I routed all the company.[1]

90 For the officers of the peace are at variance with me, and the watchman smites me with his staff.

---

[1] Dr. Johnson testified to Smart's bouts of public prayer, which are reflected in these lines.

JUBILATE AGNO

91 Let Ziba rejoice with Glottis [1] whose tongue is wreathed in his throat.

Let Micah rejoice with the spotted Spider, who counterfeits death to effect his purposes.

Let Rizpah rejoice with the Eyed Moth who is beautiful in corruption.[2]

Let Naharai, Joab's armour-bearer rejoice with Rock who is a bird of stupendous magnitude.

95 Let Abiezer, the Anethothite, rejoice with Phrynos who is the scaled frog.

Let Nachon rejoice with Parcas [3] who is a serpent more innocent than others.

Let Lapidoth with Percnos the Lord is the builder of the wall of CHINA —REJOICE.

Let Ahinoam rejoice with Prester—The seed of the woman hath bruised the serpent's head.[4]

Let Phurah rejoice with Penelopes [5] the servant of Gideon with the fowl of the brook.

100 Let Jether, the son of Gideon, rejoice with Ecchetœ which are musical grashoppers.

Let Hushai rejoice with the Ospray who is able to parry the eagle.

Let Eglah rejoice with Phalaris[6] who is a pleasant object upon the water.

Let Haggith rejoice with the white Weasel who devoureth the honey and its maker.

Let Abital rejoice with Ptyas [7] who is arrayed in green and gold.

---

[1] *Glottis*, a quail with a long tongue. *S.*
[2] *Beautiful in corruption*, that is, the wings remain beautiful after death. *S.*
[3] *Parcas* appears to be an error for Pareas, a serpent. *S.*
[4] *Prester*, a serpent whose bite caused a burning thirst. *S.* The latter part of the line echoes Gn.3.15.
[5] *Penelopes*, a kind of duck. *S.*
[6] *Phalaris*, a water-hen or coot. *S.*
[7] *Ptyas*, an adder or asp. *S.*

FRAGMENT B1

91 For I am the seed of the WELCH WOMAN [1] and speak the truth from my heart.

For they lay wagers touching my life.—God be gracious to the winners.

For the piety of Rizpah is imitable in the Lord—wherefore I pray for the dead. [2]

For the Lord is my ROCK and I am the bearer of his CROSS.

95 For I am like a frog in the brambles, but the Lord hath put his whole armour upon me.

For I was a Viper-catcher in my youth [3] and the Lord delivered me from his venom.

For I rejoice that I attribute to God, what others vainly ascribe to feeble man.

For I am ready to die for his sake—who lay down his life for all mankind.

For the son of JOSHUA shall prevail against the servant of Gideon— Good men have their betters.

100 For my seed shall worship the Lord JESUS as numerous & musical as the grashoppers of Paradise.

For I pray God to turn the council of Ahitophel into foolishness. [4]

For the learning of the Lord increases daily, as the sun is an improving angel.

For I pray God for a reformation amongst the women and the restoration of the veil.

For beauty is better to look upon than to meddle with and tis good for a man not to know a woman.

---

[1] *Welch Woman*, Smart's mother was Winifred Griffiths of Radnorshire. *S.*

[2] Rizpah mourned the hanging of her sons in 2 S.21. Stead notes that prayer for the dead was counter to post-Reformation doctrine.

[3] Smart's reference to viper-catching is to be taken literally ; see also B1.118.

[4] A paraphrase of 2 S.15.31. The counsel of Ahitophel was overthrown (2 S.17) with the aid of Hushai.

57

105 Let Maacah rejoice with Dryophyte [1] who was blessed of the Lord in the valley.

Let Zabud Solomon's friend rejoice with Oryx [2] who is a frolicksome mountaineer.

Let Adoniram the receiver general of the excise rejoice with Hypnale the sleepy adder. [3]

Let Pedahel rejoice with Pityocampa [4] who eateth his house in the pine.

Let Ibzan rejoice with the Brandling [5] the Lord further the building of bridges & making rivers navigable.

110 Let Gilead rejoice with the Gentle [6] the Lord make me a fisher of men.

Let Zelophehad rejoice with Ascalabotes [7] who casteth not his coat till a new one is prepared for him.

Let Mahlah rejoice with Pellos who is a tall bird and stately.

Let Tirzah rejoice with Tylus which is the Cheeslip and food for the chicken.

Let Hoglah rejoice with Leontophonos who will kill the lion, if he is eaten.

115 Let Milcah rejoice with the Horned Beetle who will strike a man in the face.

Let Noah rejoice with Hibris [8] who is from a wild boar and a tame sow.

---

[1] *Dryophyte*, a frog, perhaps a tree-frog. *S.*

[2] *Oryx*, a wild goat. *S.*

[3] *Hypnale*, an adder whose bite induces sleep or death. *S.* Surely the sly conjunction of the tax-collector and the sleepy adder is intentional.

[4] *Pityocampa*, the pine-caterpillar. *S.*

[5] *Brandling*, a young salmon or trout; also a bait used by anglers. *S.*

[6] *Gentle*, another fish-bait. *S.*

[7] *Ascalabotes*, a lizard. *S. Zelophehad* is followed in successive lines by her five daughters; the Noah of 116 is thus a female (Jos.17 and elsewhere) rather than the son of Lamech, who has already appeared in A4.

[8] *Hibris:* Smart is using the Greek word ὕβρις as the equivalent of the Latin *hibrida* (mongrel) applied to the mating of domestic with wild swine. *S.*

105 For the Lord Jesus made him a nosegay [1] and blessed it & and he blessed the inhabitants of flowers.

For a faithful friend is the medicine of life, but a neighbour in the Lord is better than he.

For I stood up betimes in behalf of LIBERTY, PROPERTY and NO EXCISE.

For they began with grubbing up my trees & now they have excluded the planter.

For I am the Lord's builder and free & accepted MASON in CHRIST JESUS.[2]

110 For I bless God in all gums & balsams [3] & every thing that ministers relief to the sick.

For the Sun's at work to make me a garment & the Moon is at work for my wife.[4]

For tall and stately are against me, but humiliation on humiliation is on my side.

For I have a providential acquaintance with men who bear the names of animals.

For I bless God to Mr Lion Mr Cock Mr Cat Mr Talbot Mr Hart Mrs Fysh Mr Grub, and Miss Lamb.[5]

115 For they throw my horns in my face and reptiles make themselves wings against me.

For I bless God for the immortal soul of Mr Pigg of DOWNHAM in NORFOLK.

---

[1] The *nosegay* of Christ is not Biblical and remains obscure. See also B2.494–495 and note.

[2] Smart's association with Masonry is well known; see the introduction to Stead's edition of *Jubilate Agno*, p. 25.

[3] "Choice gums and precious balm," S.D., 129.

[4] This idea is developed further in B1.192–193.

[5] These are the names of well-known families in the eastern counties, and several were represented at Cambridge in Smart's day or are among the subscribers to his works; Dame Fysh recurs in D65. S.

117 Let Abdon rejoice with the Glede [1] who is very voracious & may not himself be eaten.

Let Zuph rejoice with Dipsas,[2] whose bite causeth thirst.

Let Shechem of Manasseh rejoice with the Green Worm whose livery is of the field.

120 Let Gera rejoice with the Night Hawk blessed are those who watch when others sleep.

Let Anath rejoice with Rauca who inhabiteth the root of the oak.

Let Cherub rejoice with the Cherub who is a bird and a blessed Angel.

LET PETER rejoice with the MOON FISH who keeps up the life in the waters by night.[3]

Let Andrew rejoice with the Whale, who is arrayd in beauteous blue & is a combination of bulk & activity.

125 Let James rejoice with the Skuttle-Fish, who foils his foe by the effusion of his ink.

Let John rejoice with Nautilus who spreads his sail & plies his oar, and the Lord is his pilot.

Let Philip rejoice with Boca,[4] which is a fish that can speak.

---

[1] *Glede*, the kite. *S.*

[2] *Dipsas*, a serpent whose bite causes thirst. *S.* See the *Prester* in B1.98.

[3] Here Smart switches from the Old to the New Testament, indicating the break by a gap and special capitalization in both halves of the composition. Stead notes the appropriateness of assigning fish to these fishers of men.

[4] *Boca* : Pliny wrote *box*, corrupted by scribes and grammarians to *boca* or *bocas*, and conveniently supplied by them with the attribute of speech. *S.*

FRAGMENT B1

117 For I fast this day even the 31st of August N. S. to prepare for the SABBATH of the Lord.[1]

For the bite of an Adder is cured by its greese & the malice of my enemies by their stupidity.[2]

For I bless God in SHIPBOURNE FAIRLAWN [3] the meadows the brooks and the hills.

120 For the adversary hath exasperated the very birds against me, but the Lord sustain'd me.

For I bless God for my Newcastle friends the voice of the raven and heart of the oak.

For I bless God for every feather from the wren in the sedge to the CHERUBS & their MATES.

FOR I pray the Lord JESUS that cured the LUNATICK to be merciful to all my brethren and sisters in these houses.

For they work me with their harping-irons,[4] which is a barbarous instrument, because I am more unguarded than others.

125 For the blessing of God hath been on my epistles, which I have written for the benefit of others.

For I bless God that the CHURCH of ENGLAND is one of the SEVEN evn the candlestick of the Lord.

For the ENGLISH TONGUE shall be the language of the WEST.

[1] 31 August 1759 fell on a Friday. Of course Smart understood the Sabbath to be Saturday; see C85.

[2] Smart is recalling his youthful epigram, "On a Malignant Dull Poet" (Callan, I, 27):

> "When the viper its venom has spit, it is said,
> That its fat heals the wound which its poison has made;
> Thus it fares with the blockhead who ventures to write;
> His dullness an antidote proves to his spite."

[3] *Shipbourne* was the poet's birthplace; *Fairlawn* was Lord Vane's property in Kent. S.

[4] *Harping-iron*, a harpoon; perhaps some corrective instrument used in the asylum. S.

JUBILATE AGNO

128 Let Bartholomew rejoice with the Eel, who is pure in proportion to where he is found & how he is used.

Let Thomas rejoice with the Sword-Fish, whose aim is perpetual & strength insuperable.[1]

130 Let Matthew rejoice with Uranoscopus, whose eyes are lifted up to God.

Let James the less, rejoice with the Haddock, who brought the piece of money for the Lord and Peter.

Let Jude bless with the Bream, who is of melancholy from his depth and serenity.

Let Simon rejoice with the Sprat, who is pure and innumerable.

Let Matthias rejoice with the Flying-Fish, who has a part with the birds, and is sublimity in his conceit.

135 Let Stephen rejoice with Remora—The Lord remove all obstacles to his glory.

Let Paul rejoice with the Seale, who is pleasant & faithfull, like God's good ENGLISHMAN.

Let Agrippa, which is Agricola,[2] rejoice with Elops, who is a choice fish.

Let Joseph rejoice with the Turbut, whose capture makes the poor fisher-man sing.

Let Mary rejoice with the Maid—blessed be the name of the immaculate CONCEPTION.[3]

---

[1] Smart's transmutation of this pedestrian line (in *S.D.* 449–450) shows how the discipline of a strict form refined his art:

> "Strong through the turbulent profound
> Shoots xiphias to his aim."

[2] *Agricola* is not a Biblical name. The equation of Agrippa with Agricola and with "the steward of the island" (St. George?) is another manifestation of ideas in B1.54 and elsewhere.

[3] *Maid*, various species of skate. The end of the line evidently repeats the familiar error of confounding the Immaculate Conception of the Mother of Christ with the Virgin Birth of her Son. *S.*

FRAGMENT B1

128 For I pray Almighty CHRIST to bless the MAGDALEN HOUSE [1] & to forward a National purification.

For I have the blessing of God in the three POINTS of manhood, of the pen, of the sword, & of chivalry.

130 For I am inquisitive in the Lord, and defend the philosophy of the scripture against vain deceit.

For the nets come down from the eyes of the Lord to fish up men to their salvation.

For I have a greater compass both of mirth and melancholy than another.

For I bless the Lord JESUS in the innumerables, and for ever & ever.

For I am redoubted, and redoubtable in the Lord, as is THOMAS BECKET my father.[2]

135 For I have had the grace to GO BACK, which is my blessing unto prosperity.

For I paid for my seat in St PAUL's, when I was six years old, & took possession against the evil day.

For I am descended from the steward of the island blessed be the name of the Lord Jesus king of England.

For the poor gentleman is the first object of the Lord's charity & he is the most pitied who hath lost the most.

For I am in twelve HARDSHIPS, but he that was born of a virgin shall deliver me out of all.

[1] *Magdalen House*, an asylum for prostitutes. *S*.
[2] Probably *Becket* the famous churchman, rather than Thomas Becket the bookseller and Smart's contemporary.

140 Let John, the Baptist, rejoice with the Salmon—blessed be the name of the Lord Jesus for infant Baptism.

Let Mark rejoice with the Mullet, who is John Dore,[1] God be gracious to him & his family.

Let Barnabas rejoice with the Herring—God be gracious to the Lord's fishery.

Let Cleopas rejoice with the Mackerel, who cometh in a shoal after a leader.

Let Abiud [2] of the Lord's line rejoice with Murex, who is good and of a precious tincture.

145 Let Eliakim rejoice with the Shad, who is contemned in his abundance.

Let Azor rejoice with the Flounder, who is both of the sea and of the river.

Let Sadoc rejoice with the Bleak, who playeth upon the surface in the Sun.

Let Achim rejoice with the Miller's Thumb, who is a delicious morsel for the water fowl.

Let Eliud rejoice with Cinædus, who is a fish yellow all over.

150 Let Eleazar rejoice with the Grampus, who is a pompous spouter.

Let Matthan rejoice with the Shark, who is supported by multitudes of small value.

Let Jacob rejoice with the Gold Fish, who is an eye-trap.

---

[1] *John Dore*, an inmate of St. Luke's and Bethlehem Hospitals during Smart's confinement; associated with the fish, *John Dore*. S.

[2] The names from Abiud to Eleazar are taken in order from the genealogy of Joseph in Mt.1.13–16.

140 For I am safe, as to my head, from the female dancer and her admirers.[1]

For I pray for CHICHESTER to give the glory to God, and to keep the adversary at bay.

For I am making to the shore day by day, the Lord Jesus take me.

For I bless the Lord JESUS upon RAMSGATE PIER—the Lord forward the building of harbours.

For I bless the Lord JESUS for his very seed, which is in my body.

145 For I pray for R and his family, I pray for Mr Becher, and I bean for the Lord JESUS.[2]

For I pray to God for Nore, for the Trinity house, for all light-houses, beacons and buoys.[3]

For I bless God that I am not in a dungeon, but am allowed the light of the Sun.

For I pray God for the PYGMIES against their featherd adversaries, as a deed of charity.

For I pray God for all those, who have defiled themselves in matters inconvenient.

150 For I pray God be gracious to CORNELIUS MATTHEWS name & connection.

For I am under the same accusation with my Saviour—for they said, he is besides himself.[4]

For I pray God for the introduction of new creatures into this island.

---

[1] The *female dancer* is Salome, whose name may have suggested the Salmon as the appropriate fish to link with John the Baptist.

[2] *R and his family* may possibly be read *Rand his family*, or it may stand for *Rain and his family* as in C97. *Bean* may be connected with the noun *bene*, a prayer; but *N.E.D.* does not record its use as a verb.

[3] The first Nore light was erected in 1731. *S.*

[4] A quotation of Mk.3.21.

JUBILATE AGNO

153 Let Jairus rejoice with the Silver Fish, who is bright & lively.

Let Lazarus rejoice with Torpedo, who chills the life of the assailant through his staff.[1]

155 Let Mary Magdalen rejoice with the Place, whose goodness & purity are of the Lord's making.

Let Simon the leper rejoice with the Eel-pout, who is a rarity on account of his subtlety.

Let Alpheus rejoice with the Whiting, whom God hath blessed in multitudes, & his days are as the days of PURIM.[2]

Let Onesimus rejoice with the Cod—blessed be the name of the Lord Jesus for a miraculous draught of men.

Let Joses rejoice with the Sturgeon, who saw his maker in the body and obtained grace.

160 Let Theophilus rejoice with the Folio, who hath teeth, like the teeth of a saw.

Let Bartimæus [3] rejoice with the Quaviver—God be gracious to the eyes of him, who prayeth for the blind.

Let CHRISTOPHER, who is Simon of Cyrene,[4] rejoice with the Rough —God be gracious to the CAM & to DAVID CAM & his seed for ever.

Let Timæus rejoice with the Ling—God keep the English Sailors clear of French bribery.

---

[1] *Torpedo*, "that extraordinary fish . . . whoever handles it, or happens even to set his foot upon it, is presently seized with a numbness all over him," Anson, p. 266. *S.* Smart was clearly thinking of Anson's account, for the phrase *chills the life of the assailant through his staff* refers to Anson's anecdote in the same passage, where he tells how he received a shock from a torpedo through his walking-stick. This incident was cited in *The Student*, I (1750), 51, in a footnote to an article by J. Ingram entitled "New Experiments concerning the TORPEDO." In the Biblical reference Smart confuses the Lazarus of the parable (Lk.16) with the Lazarus who was raised from the dead.

[2] *Purim*, an annual two-day feast commemorating the deliverance of the Jews from Haman.

[3] *Bartimæus*, the blind beggar of Jericho whose sight was restored, Mk.10.46.

[4] *Christopher* is not a Biblical name; but Simon of Cyrene was forced to bear the cross after Christ, and so the appellation is in some wise appropriate to him.

66

FRAGMENT B1

153 For I pray God for the ostriches of Salisbury Plain, the beavers of the Medway & silver fish of Thames.[1]

For Charity is cold in the multitude of possessions, & the rich are covetous of their crumbs.[2]

155 For I pray to be accepted as a dog without offence, which is best of all.

For I wish to God and desire towards the most High, which is my policy.

For the tides are the life of God in the ocean, and he sends his angel to trouble the great DEEP.

For he hath fixed the earth upon arches & pillars, and the flames of hell flow under it.[3]

For the grosser the particles the nearer to the sink, & the nearer to purity, the quicker the gravitation.

160 For MATTER is the dust of the Earth, every atom of which is the life.

For MOTION is as the quantity of life direct, & that which hath not motion, is resistance.

For Resistance is not of GOD, but he—hath built his works upon it.

For the Centripetal and Centrifugal forces are GOD SUSTAINING and DIRECTING.[4]

[1] The ostriches of Salisbury Plain were large bustards, and beavers were once indigenous in the British Isles; see the letter of Allen W. Seaby in *Times Literary Supplement*, 17 February 1950, p. 105. There were many attempts to domesticate exotic fish in British waters.

[2] From this point on, the relationship between *Let* and *For* verses rapidly deteriorates. Each section tends to go its own way, with only occasional and rather tenuous correspondence.

[3] This notion appears to spring from the Seven Pillars of Wisdom in Prov.9.1, as embroidered and expanded by cabbalistic and hermetic writers. In *S.D.* Smart construes the Seven Pillars as the seven days of the Creation.

[4] Stead points out that some of the scientific notions here and elsewhere in the poem resemble those in Derham's *Astro-Theology* and *Physico-Theology*, works extremely influential in eighteenth-century thought. The extent of this parallelism may be judged from the analysis of Derham's conclusions given by Basil Willey in *The Eighteenth Century Background* (London, 1940), p. 42: "God did not spend so much skill on his creatures to have them ignored; it is our pious duty, therefore, as well as our interest, to study Nature."

Let Salome rejoice with the Mermaid, who hath the countenance & a portion of human reason.

165 Let Zacharias rejoice with the Gudgeon, who improves in his growth till he is mistaken.

Let Campanus rejoice with the Lobster—God be gracious to all the CAMPBELLs especially John.[1]

Let Martha rejoice with the Skallop—the Lord revive the exercise and excellence of the Needle.

Let Mary rejoice with the Carp—the ponds of Fairlawn [2] and the garden bless for the master.

Let Zebedee rejoice with the Tench—God accept the good son for his parents also.

170 Let Joseph of Arimathea rejoice with the Barbel—a good coffin and a tomb-stone without grudging! [3]

Let Elizabeth rejoice with the Crab—it is good, at times, to go back.

Let Simeon rejoice with the Oyster, who hath the life without locomotion.

Let Jona rejoice with the Wilk—Wilks, Wilkie, and Wilkinson bless the name of the Lord Jesus.

Let Nicodemus rejoice with the Muscle,[4] for so he hath provided for the poor.

175 Let Gamaliel rejoice with the Cockle—I will rejoice in the remembrance of mercy.

---

[1] *Campanus* is not a Biblical name and no good reason has been found for its intrusion here. *John Campbell* was probably the 2nd Duke of Argyll (d. 1743), on whom Smart published the following epitaph in his *Ode to the . . . Earl of Northumberland* (Callan, I, 37):

> "To Death's grim shades let meaner spirits fly,
> Here rests JOHN CAMPBELL, who shall never die."

[2] *Fairlawn*, see B1.119.
[3] Jesus was interred in the sepulchre belonging to Joseph of Arimathea, Mt.27.57 ff.
[4] *Muscle*, mussel.

FRAGMENT B1

For Elasticity is the temper of matter to recover its place with vehemence.

165 For Attraction is the earning of parts, which have a similitude in the life.[1]

For the Life of God is in the Loadstone, and there is a magnet, which pointeth due EAST.[2]

For the Glory of God is always in the East, but cannot be seen for the cloud of the crucifixion.

For due East is the way to Paradise, which man knoweth not by reason of his fall.

For the Longitude is (nevertheless) attainable by steering angularly notwithstanding.[3]

170 For Eternity is a creature & is built upon Eternity καταβολη επι τη διαβολη.[4]

For Fire is a mixed nature of body & spirit, & the body is fed by that which hath not life.[5]

For Fire is exasperated by the Adversary, who is Death, unto the detriment of man.

For an happy Conjecture is a miraculous cast by the Lord Jesus.

For a bad Conjecture is a draught of stud and mud.[6]

175 For there is a Fire which is blandishing, and which is of God direct.

[1] *Earn* is a legitimate eighteenth-century variant of *yearn* (see *N.E.D.*) and Smart uses it again in B2.674. The concept of the attraction and sympathy of similars underlies much of Smart's natural philosophy; see also the ascent of water and vapours (B1.205), the barometer (B1.213), and so forth.
[2] To the mystics, the *magnet* pointing due East would be the heart of the worshipper. *S.*
[3] The problem of determining the longitude much exercised eighteenth-century mathematicians, and many attempted solutions were advanced in response to various prizes offered by the Royal Society and other organizations. The particular solutions referred to here and in B1.190 are obscure and have not been identified.
[4] The Greek phrase means: a foundation on slander (Satan?). *S.*
[5] As Stead points out, this fire is not actual, but the spiritual fire of the hermetic philosophers.
[6] *Stud and mud*, lath plastered with clay; Smart evidently meant only *mud*, but could not resist the jingle of the familiar North-country builders' phrase. *S.*

176 Let Agabus rejoice with the Smelt—The Lord make me serviceable to the HOWARDs.

Let Rhoda rejoice with the Sea-Cat, who is pleasantry and purity.

Let Elmodam rejoice with the Chubb, who is wary of the bait & thrives in his circumspection.

Let Jorim rejoice with the Roach—God bless my throat [1] & keep me from things stranggled.

180 Let Addi rejoice with the Dace—It is good to angle with meditation.[2]

Let Luke rejoice with the Trout—Blessed be Jesus in Aa, in Dee [3] and in Isis.

Let Cosam rejoice with the Perch, who is a little tyrant, because he is not liable to that, which he inflicts.

Let Levi rejoice with the Pike—God be merciful to all dumb creatures in respect of pain.

Let Melchi rejoice with the Char, who cheweth the cud.

185 Let Joanna rejoice with the Anchovy—I beheld and lo! a great multitude! [4]

Let Neri rejoice with the Keeling Fish, who is also called the Stock Fish.

---

[1] *God bless my throat* is the earliest of a series of references which suggest that Smart suffered from chronic respiratory infection, if not from tuberculosis. See also B1.225, C68–70, C74, C100, and D125.

[2] The sub-title of Izaak Walton's *Compleat Angler* is *The Contemplative Man's Recreation*; the fish in lines 178–184 are all discussed by Walton.

[3] *In Aa, in Dee* probably derives from the name *Addi* in the line preceding.

[4] *Joanna* also occurs in B1.198, again coupled with the idea of small fish in great numbers. There appear to be no Biblical grounds for such an association. The latter part of the line is quoted from Rev.7.9. An interesting example of the way Smart's mind seemed to divide things into categories is to be seen in his citation in this and the succeeding lines of fish which are preserved by smoking, salting, or drying.

FRAGMENT B1

176 For Fire is a substance and distinct, and purifyeth evn in hell.

For the Shears is the first of the mechanical powers, and to be used on the knees.[1]

For if Adam had used this instrument right, he would not have fallen.

For the power of the Shears is direct as the life.

180 For the power of the WEDGE is direct as it's altitude by communication of Almighty God.[2]

For the Skrew, Axle & Wheel, Pulleys, the Lever & inclined Plane are known in the Schools.

For the Centre is not known but by the application of the members to matter.

For I have shown the Vis Inertiæ to be false, and such is all nonsense.[3]

For the Centre is the hold of the Spirit upon the matter in hand.

185 For FRICTION is inevitable because the Universe is FULL of God's works.[4]

For the PERPETUAL MOTION is in all the works of Almighty GOD.

---

[1] The reference to *shears* may imply Smart's familiarity with the ancient divination "by the sieve and shears." *S.* But he may only be likening the tailor's traditional posture to the attitude of adoration, a matter of importance to him; see, for example, C108–109. Rev. Christopher Hunter reports in the *Poems* (1791), I, xxviii, "Mr. Smart, in composing the religious poems, was frequently so impressed with the sentiment of devotion, as to write particular passages on his knees."

[2] The passage beginning here suggests that Smart had been reading something on mechanics and physics and was trying to give the objects mentioned a spiritual meaning. *S.*

[3] *Vis Inertiæ* as referred to here is probably a reminiscence of Smart's Cambridge Tripos poem, "Materies gaudet vi inertiæ," translated as "The Temple of Dulness." See Smart's *Poems* (1791), II, 139–149; and also below, B1.227.

[4] The multitude in the *Let* verse is echoed by the multiplicity of God's works, showing that a tenuous relationship still obtains between the two parts. But mostly each pursues its own themes.

187 Let Janna rejoice with the Pilchard—the Lord restore the seed of Abishai.

Let Esli rejoice with the Soal, who is flat and spackles for the increase of motion.[1]

Let Nagge rejoice with the Perriwinkle—"for the rain it raineth every day." [2]

190 Let Anna rejoice with the Porpus, who is a joyous fish and of good omen.

Let Phanuel rejoice with the Shrimp, which is the childrens fishery.

Let Chuza rejoice with the Sea-Bear,[3] who is full of sagacity and prank.

Let Susanna rejoice with the Lamprey, who is an eel with a title.

Let Candace rejoice with the Craw-fish—How hath the Christian minister renowned the Queen.[4]

195 Let The Eunuch rejoice with the Thorn-Back—It is good to be discovered reading the BIBLE.

Let Simon the Pharisee rejoice with the Grigg—the Lord bring up Issachar and Dan.

Let Simon the converted Sorcerer rejoice with the Dab quoth Daniel.

Let Joanna,[5] of the Lord's line, rejoice with the Minnow, who is multiplied against the oppressor.

---

[1] *Soal* is an archaic spelling of *sole* (not *seal*, as Stead suggests). The verb *spackles* is unknown to *N.E.D.*, which records an adverb *spackly* meaning speedily; this may be what Smart had in mind.

[2] Smart quotes Shakespeare suddenly; the profusion of winkles reminds him of the raindrops without number. S.

[3] *Sea-Bear*, either the polar bear or the fur seal. S.

[4] *Candace* is "renowned" (Ac.8.26–40) only because her treasurer was discovered by Philip in the act of reading Isaiah, and was baptized by him. This treasurer is *The Eunuch* of the next line.

[5] *Joanna*, see B1.185.

FRAGMENT B1

187 For it is not so in the engines of man, which are made of dead materials, neither indeed can be.

For the Moment of bodies, as it is used, is a false term—bless God ye Speakers on the Fifth of November.

For Time and Weight are by their several estimates.

190 For I bless GOD in the discovery of the LONGITUDE direct by the means of GLADWICK.[1]

For the motion of the PENDULUM is the longest in that it parries resistance.

For the WEDDING GARMENTS of all men are prepared in the SUN against the day of acceptation.

For the Wedding Garments of all women are prepared in the MOON against the day of their purification.[2]

For CHASTITY is the key of knowledge as in Esdras, Sr Isaac Newton & now, God be praised, in me.

195 For Newton nevertheless is more of error than of the truth, but I am of the WORD of GOD.

For WATER is not of solid constituents, but is dissolved from precious stones above.

For the life remains in its dissolvent state, and that in great power.

For WATER is condensed by the Lord's FROST, tho' not by the FLORENTINE experiment.[3]

---

[1] See also B1.169. *Gladwick* has not been identified; its description (B1.199–203) suggests mica, which was also known as glimmer, glist, Muscovy glass, etc. It might also be some kind of spar whose power of refraction would make it useful in optical instruments; but a search of mineralogical literature has so far failed to reveal a substance bearing this or a similar name.

[2] This and the preceding line were foreshadowed in B1.111.

[3] *Florentine experiment* appears to refer to the experiments in artificial refrigeration reported in the late seventeenth century by the Accademia del Cimento in Florence.

JUBILATE AGNO

Let Jonas rejoice with the Sea-Devil, who hath a good[1] name from his Maker.

200 Let Alexander [2] rejoice with the Tunny—the worse the time the better the eternity.

Let Rufus [3] rejoice with the Needle-fish, who is very good in his element.

Let Matthat rejoice with the Trumpet-fish—God revive the blowing of the TRUMPETS.

Let Mary, the mother of James, rejoice with the Sea-Mouse it is good to be at peace.

Let Prochorus rejoice with Epodes,[4] who is a kind of fish with Ovid who is at peace in the Lord.

205 Let Timotheus rejoice with the Dolphin, who is of benevolence.

Let Nicanor rejoice with the Skeat—Blessed be the name of the Lord Jesus in fish and in the Shewbread, which ought to be continually on the altar, now more than ever, and the want of it is the Abomination of Desolation spoken of by Daniel.[5]

Let Timon rejoice with Crusion—The Shew-Bread in the first place is gratitude to God to shew who is bread,[6] whence it is, and that there is enough and to spare.

Let Parmenas rejoice with the Mixon—secondly it is to prevent the last extremity, for it is lawful that rejected hunger may take it.[7]

---

[1] *Good* must be taken as meaning "appropriate" here; Smart often avoids the word Devil, preferring Adversary. *S.*

[2] *Alexander* reappears at B1.233.

[3] *Rufus* reappears at B1.252.

[4] *Epodes*, a flat fish in the Pontus, mentioned in Ovid's *Halieuticon. S.*

[5] *The abomination of desolation, spoken of by Daniel* comes from Mt.24.15 or Mk.13.14, which in turn refer to Dan.11.31 and 12.11. Coupling this with the absence of shewbread from the altar appears to be Smart's personal interpretation of the latter verse. The shewbread consisted of twelve unleavened loaves, eaten by the priests after a week's exposure on the altar, at which time twelve new loaves replaced them.

[6] Smart's derivation of the term *shewbread* is purely fanciful.

[7] The shewbread was eaten to assuage hunger by Daniel and his companions at Nob (1 S.21.3–6).

74

FRAGMENT B1

For GLADWICK is a substance growing on hills in the East, candied by the sun, and of diverse colours.[1]

200 For it is neither stone nor metal but a new creature, soft to the ax, but hard to the hammer.

For it answers sundry uses, but particularly it supplies the place of Glass.

For it giveth a benign light without the fragility, malignity or mischief of Glass.

For it attracteth all the colours of the GREAT BOW which is fixed in the EAST.

For the FOUNTAINS and SPRINGS are the life of the waters working up to God.

205 For they are in SYMPATHY with the waters above the Heavens, which are solid.[2]

For the Fountains, springs and rivers are all of them from the sea, whose water is filtrated and purified by the earth.

For there is Water above the visible surface in a spiritualizing state, which cannot be seen but by application of a CAPILLARY TUBE.

For the ASCENT of VAPOURS is the return of thanksgiving from all humid bodies.

[1] See note on B1.190.
[2] Smart earlier stated the basis for this line of reasoning about certain natural phenomena, in B1.165.

JUBILATE AGNO

Let Dorcas rejoice with Dracunculus—blessed be the name of the Lord Jesus in the Grotto.

210 Let Tychicus rejoice with Scolopendra, who quits himself of the hook by voiding his intrails.

Let Trophimus rejoice with the Sea-Horse,[1] who shoud have been to Tychicus the father of Yorkshiremen.

Let Tryphena rejoice with Fluta—Saturday is the Sabbath for the mouth of God hath spoken it.

Let Tryphosa rejoice with Acarne—with such preparation the Lord's Jubile is better kept.

Let Simon the Tanner rejoice with Alausa—Five days are sufficient for the purposes of husbandry.

215 Let Simeon Niger rejoice with the Loach—The blacks are the seed of Cain.

Let Lucius rejoice with Corias—Some of Cain's seed was preserved in the loins of Ham at the flood.

Let Manaen rejoice with Donax. My DEGREE is good even here, in the Lord I have a better.

Let Sergius Paulus rejoice with Dentex—Blessed be the name Jesus for my teeth.

Let Silas rejoice with the Cabot the philosophy of the times evn now is vain deceit.

220 Let Barsabas rejoice with Cammarus—Newton is ignorant for if a man consult not the WORD how should he understand the WORK?—

Let Lydia rejoice with Attilus—Blessed be the name of him which eat the fish & honey comb.[2]

Let Jason rejoice with Alopecias,[3] who is subtlety without offence.

---

[1] *Sea-horse* may refer to the walrus rather than the creature usually known by this name. Smart's statement that he intended to allot the sea-horse to Tychicus, named in the preceding line, implies that he had some scheme of arrangement. Tychicus suggests "Yorkshire Tykes." S.

[2] *Him which eat the fish & honey comb* is the resurrected Christ, Lk.24.42–43.

[3] Striking remains of an alphabetical arrangement may be seen in the names of fish appearing in the next seventy-odd lines.

FRAGMENT B1

For the RAIN WATER kept in a reservoir at any altitude, suppose of a thousand feet will make a fountain from a spout of ten feet of the same height.

210 For it will ascend in a stream two thirds of the way and afterwards prank itself into ten thousand agreeable forms.

For the SEA is a seventh of the Earth—the spirit of the Lord by Esdras.

For MERCURY is affected by the AIR because it is of a similar subtlety.

For the rising in the BAROMETER is not effected by pressure but by sympathy.

For it cannot be seperated from the creature with which it is intimately & eternally connected.

215 For where it is stinted of air there it will adhere together & stretch on the reverse.

For it works by ballancing according to the hold of the spirit.

For QUICK-SILVER is spiritual and so is the AIR to all intents and purposes.

For the AIR-PUMP weakens & dispirits but cannot wholly exhaust.

For SUCKTION is the withdrawing of the life, but life will follow as fast as it can.

220 For there is infinite provision to keep up the life in all the parts of Creation.

For the AIR is contaminated by curses and evil language.

For poysonous creatures catch some of it & retain it or ere it goes to the adversary.

223 Let Dionysïus rejoice with Alabes who is peculiar to the Nile.

Let Damaris rejoice with Anthias—The fountain of the Nile is known to the Eastern people who drink it.

225 Let Apollos rejoice with Astacus, but St Paul is the Agent for England.[1]

Let Justus [2] rejoice with Crispus in a Salmon-Trout—the Lord look on the soul of Richard Atwood.

Let Crispus rejoice with Leviathan—God be gracious to the soul of HOBBES, who was no atheist, but a servant of Christ, and died in the Lord—I wronged him God forgive me.[3]

Let Aquila rejoice with Beemoth who is Enoch no fish but a stupendous creeping Thing.

Let Priscilla rejoice with Cythera. As earth increases by Beemoth so the sea likewise enlarges.

230 Let Tyrannus rejoice with Cephalus who hath a great head.

Let Gaius rejoice with the Water-Tortoise—Paul & Tychicus were in England with Agricola my father.[4]

Let Aristarchus rejoice with Cynoglossus—The Lord was at Glastonbury in ye body and blessed the thorn.[5]

Let Alexander rejoice with the Sea-Urchin—The Lord was at Bristol & blessed the waters there.

Let Sopater rejoice with Elacate—The waters of Bath were blessed by St Matthias.

235 Let Secundus rejoice with Echeneis who is the sea-lamprey.

---

[1] St. Paul as the *Agent for England* remains unexplained; possibly Smart is thinking of St. Paul's Cathedral.

[2] *Justus* reappears in B1.281.

[3] Once again Smart recalls his old Tripos poem, "Materies gaudet vi inertiæ," where in the Temple of Dulness he linked Hobbes with Epicurus, Spinoza, and other "atheists." See *Poems* (1791), II, 142–143.

[4] *Paul & Tychicus were in England*, see B1.225 and B1.210–211. *Agricola my father*, see B1.137.

[5] The *Glastonbury Thorn* was said to have been planted by Joseph of Arimathea. The references to Christ and Matthias in England in this and succeeding lines remain unexplained.

223 For IRELAND was without these creatures, till of late, because of the simplicity of the people.

For the AIR is purified by prayer which is made aloud and with all our might.[1]

225 For loud prayer is good for weak lungs and for a vitiated throat.

For SOUND is propagated in the spirit and in all directions.

For the VOICE of a figure is compleat in all its parts.

For a man speaks HIMSELF from the crown of his head to the sole of his feet.

For a LION roars HIMSELF compleat from head to tail.

230 For all these things are seen in the spirit which makes the beauty of prayer.

For all whispers and unmusical sounds in general are of the Adversary.

For "I will hiss saith the Lord" [2] is God's denunciation of death.

For applause [3] or the clapping of the hands is the natural action of a man on the descent of the glory of God.

For EARTH which is an intelligence hath a voice and a propensity to speak in all her parts.

235 For ECHO is the soul of the voice exerting itself in hollow places.

[1] This is not the only place where Smart advocates loud prayer; see B1.89.
[2] *I will hiss saith the Lord* appears to be an imperfect recollection of Is.5.26.
[3] *Applause*: for Smart's interpretation see also B2.343 and *S.D.* 115–117:

> "Of man—the semblance and effect
> Of God and Love—the Saint elect
> For infinite applause——"

236 Let Eutychus [1] rejoice with Cnide—Fish and honeycomb are blessed to eat after a recovery.—

Let Mnason rejoice with Vulvula a sort of fish—Good words are of God, the cant from the Devil.

Let Claudius Lysias rejoice with Coracinus who is black and peculiar to Nile.

Let Bernice rejoice with Corophium which is a kind of crab.

240 Let Phebe rejoice with Echinometra who is a beautiful shellfish red & green.

Let Epenetus rejoice with Erythrinus who is red with a white belly.

Let Andronicus rejoice with Esox, the Lax, a great fish of the Rhine.

Let Junia rejoice with the Faber-Fish—Broild fish & honeycomb may be taken for the sacrament. [2]

Let Amplias rejoice with Garus, who is a kind of Lobster.

245 Let Urbane rejoice with Glanis, who is a crafty fish who bites away the bait & saves himself.

Let Stachys rejoice with Glauciscus, who is good for Women's milk.

Let Apelles rejoice with Glaucus—behold the seed of the brave & ingenious how they are saved!

Let Aristobulus rejoice with Glycymerides who is pure and sweet.

Let Herodion rejoice with Holothuria which are prickly fishes.

[1] *Eutychus* was restored to life by Paul (Ac.20.9–12), suggesting once more to Smart the food of the resurrected Christ (B1.221).

[2] *Fish & honeycomb*, see B1.221 and B1.236.

FRAGMENT B1

236 For ECHO cannot act but when she can parry the adversary.

For ECHO is greatest in Churches and where she can assist in prayer.

For a good voice hath its Echo with it and it is attainable by much supplication.

For the VOICE is from the body and the spirit—and is a body and a spirit.

240 For the prayers of good men are therefore visible to second-sighted persons.

For HARPSICHORDS are best strung with gold wire.

For HARPS and VIOLS are best strung with Indian weed.[1]

For the GERMAN FLUTE is an indirect—the common flute good, bless the Lord Jesus BENJAMIN HALLET.[2]

For the feast of TRUMPETS [3] should be kept up, that being the most direct & acceptable of all instruments.

245 For the TRUMPET of God is a blessed intelligence & so are all the instruments in HEAVEN.

For GOD the father Almighty plays upon the HARP of stupendous magnitude and melody.

For innumerable Angels fly out at every touch and his tune is a work of creation.

For at that time malignity ceases and the devils themselves are at peace.

For this time is perceptible to man by a remarkable stillness and serenity of soul.

---

[1] *Indian weed*, also known as Indian grass, a term used in the seventeenth and eighteenth centuries for silkworm gut.

[2] Here the poet differentiates between the newer transverse (German) flute and the recorder or fipple flute. Smart had mentioned Hallet in *The Midwife* in 1753 (p. 61) as "A Child not nine Years Old, who plays admirably upon the Violencello, and in every other Respect has a Capacity greatly beyond his Years."

[3] *The feast of trumpets* was the most important Jewish new-moon festival.

250 Let Narcissus rejoice with Hordeia [1] I will magnify the Lord who multi-plied the fish.

Let Persis rejoice with Liparis I will magnify the Lord who multiplied the barley loaves.

Let Rufus rejoice with Icthyocolla of whose skin a water-glue is made.

Let Asyncritus rejoice with Labrus who is a voracious fish. [2]

Let Phlegon rejoice with the Sea-Lizard—Bless Jesus THOMAS BOWLBY & all the seed of Reuben.

255 Let Hermas rejoice with Lamyrus who is of things creeping in the sea.

Let Patrobas rejoice with Lepas, all shells are precious.

Let Hermes rejoice with Lepus, who is a venomous fish.

Let Philologus rejoice with Ligarius—shells are all parries to the adversary.

Let Julia rejoice with the Sleeve-Fish—Blessed be Jesus for all the TAYLERS.

260 Let Nereus rejoice with the Calamary—God give success to our fleets.

Let Olympas rejoice with the Sea-Lantern, which glows upon the waters.

Let Sosipater rejoice with Cornuta. there are fish for the Sea-Night-Birds that glow at bottom.

Let Lucius rejoice with the Cackrel Fish. God be gracious to Mr FLETCHER who has my tackling.

---

[1] *Hordeia* suggested *horde* to Smart, who was perpetually awed by the multiplicity of God's works.

[2] *Labrus, a voracious fish* represents a confusion in Smart's mind between *labrus*, a Plinean fish described as having "a pleasant tail," and either the Greek word λάβρος, greedy, or *Labros*, a voracious dog in Ovid. *S.*

250 For the Æolian harp is improveable into regularity.

For when it is so improved it will be known to be the SHAWM.

For it woud be better if the LITURGY were musically performed.

For the strings of the SHAWM were upon a cylinder which turned to the wind.

For this was spiritual musick altogether, as the wind is a spirit.

255 For there is nothing but it may be played upon in delight.

For the flames of fire may be blown thro musical pipes.[1]

For it is so higher up in the vast empyrean.

For nothing is so real as that which is spiritual.

For an IGNIS FATUUS is either the fool's conceit or a blast from the adversary.

260 For SHELL-FIRE [2] or ELECTRICAL is the quick air when it is caught.

For GLASS is worked in the fire till it partakes of its nature.

For the electrical fire is easily obtain'd by the working of glass.

For all spirits are of fire and the air is a very benign one.

---

[1] "The fact that a jet of hydrogen, burning in an open tube, would under certain conditions cause a musical note to be emitted, was first observed by Higgens in 1777, and other observers studied various aspects of the phenomenon," E. G. Richardson, *Sound, a Physical Textbook* (3rd ed., London, 1940), p. 197. It may not be too much to suppose that Smart had witnessed or heard of earlier experiments along the same line.

[2] *Shell-fire*, the phosphorescence sometimes exhibited in farmyards from decayed straw, etc. *S*. Smart connects it with static electricity.

JUBILATE AGNO

Let Tertius rejoice with Maia which is a kind of crab.

265 Let Erastis rejoice with Melandry which is the largest Tunny.

Let Quartus rejoice with Mena. God be gracious to the immortal soul of poor Carte, who was barbarously & cowardly murder'd [1]—the Lord prevent the dealers in clandestine death.

Let Sosthenes rejoice with the Winkle—all shells like the parts of the body are good kept for those parts.

Let Chloe rejoice with the Limpin—There is a way to the terrestrial Paradise upon the knees. [2]

Let Carpus rejoice with the Frog-Fish—A man cannot die upon his knees.

270 Let Stephanas rejoice with Mormyra who is a fish of divers colours.

Let Fortunatus rejoice with the Burret [3]—it is good to be born when things are crossed.

Let Lois rejoice with the Angel-Fish—There is a fish that swims in the fluid Empyrean.

Let Achaicus rejoice with the Fat-Back—The Lord invites his fishers to the WEST INDIES.

Let Silvanus rejoice with the Black-Fish—Oliver Cromwell himself was the murderer in the Mask. [4]

275 Let Titus rejoice with Mys—O Tite siquid ego adjuero curamve levasso! [5]

---

[1] *Poor Carte, who was barbarously murder'd*—in the MS., followed by the deleted words *by Atterbury*. Thomas Carte (1686–1754) is said to have acted as secretary to Francis Atterbury, bishop of Rochester (1662–1732). Carte fled before the anti-Jacobite storm that engulfed Atterbury in 1722, but he was not murdered, and indeed he survived Atterbury.

[2] This pair of lines is one of the very few examples of correlation between *Let* and *For* verses in this part of the poem.

[3] *Burret* is the murex, already cited in B1.144.

[4] *The murderer in the Mask* is a reference to the masked executioner of Charles I. *S.* Smart evidently had pronounced Jacobite sympathies; see B1.71.

[5] The Latin tag means: O Titus, if in anything I have helped you or eased your care. *S.*

For the MAN in VACUO is a flat conceit of preposterous folly.

265 For the breath of our nostrils is an electrical spirit.

For an electrical spirit may be exasperated into a malignant fire.

For it is good to quicken in paralytic cases being the life applied unto death.[1]

For the method of philosophizing is in a posture of Adoration.

For the School-Doctrine of Thunder & Lightning is a Diabolical Hypothesis.[2]

270 For it is taking the nitre from the lower regions and directing it against the Infinite of Heights.

For THUNDER is the voice of God direct in verse and musick.

For LIGHTNING is a glance of the glory of God.

For the Brimstone that is found at the times of thunder & lightning is worked up by the Adversary.

For the voice is always for infinite good which he strives to impede.

275 For the Devil can work coals into shapes to afflict the minds of those that will not pray.

---

[1] Benjamin Franklin contributed a paper on "The Effects of Electricity in Paralytic Cases" to *Philosophical Transactions*, 1758, p. 481; and other investigations were going forward on similar lines. *S.*

[2] The identification of lightning with electricity was still hypothetical. *S.*

JUBILATE AGNO

276 Let Euodias rejoice with Myrcus—There is a perfumed fish I will offer him for a sweet savour to the Lord.

Let Syntyche rejoice with Myax—There are shells in the earth which were left by the FLOOD.[1]

Let Clement rejoice with Ophidion—There are shells again in earth at sympathy with those in sea.

Let Epaphroditus rejoice with Ophthalmias—The Lord increase the Cambridge collection of fossils.[2]

280 Let Epaphras rejoice with Orphus—God be gracious to the immortal soul of Dr Woodward.

Let Justus rejoice with Pagrus—God be gracious to the immortal soul of Dr Middleton.

Let Nymphas rejoice with Pagurus—God bless Charles Mason & all Trinity College.

Let Archippus rejoice with Nerita whose shell swimmeth.

Let Eunice rejoice with Oculata who is of the Lizard kind.

285 Let Onesiphorus rejoice with Orca, who is a great fish.

Let Eubulus rejoice with Ostrum ye scarlet [3] God be gracious to Gordon & Groat.

Let Pudens rejoice with Polypus—The Lord restore my virgin!

Let Linus rejoice with Ozæna who is a kind of Polype—God be gracious to Lyne & Anguish.

---

[1] Smart shared the contemporary interest in fossils—a term which then included anything found in the ground, not merely the remains and traces of organic matter which we today understand as fossils.

[2] After mentioning *the Cambridge collection of fossils*, Smart proceeds to name in succeeding lines John Woodward (1665–1728) the geologist and founder of the Woodwardian Chair at Cambridge, followed by two later Cambridge geologists, Conyers Middleton (1683–1750) and Charles Mason (d. 1771). *S.*

[3] *Ostrum*, another name for murex; *ye scarlet* applies to Ostrum. *S.*

FRAGMENT B1

276 For the coffin and the cradle and the purse are all against a man.[1]

For the coffin is for the dead and death came by disobedience.

For the cradle is for weakness and the child of man was originally strong from ye womb.

For the purse is for money and money is dead matter with the stamp of human vanity.

280 For the adversary frequently sends these particular images out of the fire to those whom they concern.

For the coffin is for me because I have nothing to do with it.

For the cradle is for me because the old Dragon attacked me in it & I overcame in Christ.[2]

For the purse is for me because I have neither money nor human friends.

For LIGHT is propagated at all distances in an instant because it is actuated by the divine conception.

285 For the Satellites of the planet prove nothing in this matter but the glory of Almighty God.

For the SHADE is of death and from the adversary.[3]

For Solomon said vanity of vanities vanity of vanities all is vanity.

For Jesus says verity of verities verity of verities all is verity.

---

[1] These references to *the coffin and the cradle and the purse* remain unexplained, although Smart evidently felt them to have some personal significance.
[2] *The Old Dragon attacked me in* [*the cradle*], a reference to Smart's ill-health in infancy. *S.*
[3] See B2.308.

JUBILATE AGNO

Let Claudia rejoice with Pascer [1]—the purest creatures minister to wantoness by unthankfulness.

290 Let Artemas rejoice with Pastinaca who is a fish with a sting.

Let Zenas rejoice with Pecten—The Lord obliterate the laws of man! [2]

Let Philemon rejoice with Pelagia—The laws & judgement are impudence & blindness.

Let Apphia rejoice with Pelamis—The Lord Jesus is man's judgement.

Let Demetrius rejoice with Peloris, who is greatest of Shell-Fishes.

295 Let Antipas rejoice with Pentadactylus—A papist hath no sentiment God bless CHURCHILL. [3]

---

[1] *Pascer*, a fish in Ovid's *Halieuticon. S.* This may have suggested *passer*, sparrow, a classic symbol of lasciviousness.

[2] Here again the *Let* and *For* verses come into something like their earlier relationship.

[3] *Churchill* is evidently Charles Churchill, the poet (1731–1764); Smart must have known him when he was comparatively obscure, as his fame dated from the *Rosciad* (1761). *S.* See D62, note.

FRAGMENT B1

For Solomon said THOU FOOL in malice from his own vanity.

290 For the Lord reviled not at all in hardship and temptation unutterable.

For Fire hath this property that it reduces a thing till finally it is not.

For all the filth of wicked men shall be done away by fire in Eternity.

For the furnace itself shall come up at the last according to Abraham's vision.[1]

For the Convex of Heaven [2] shall work about on that great event.

295 For the ANTARTICK POLE is not yet but shall answer in the Consummation.

[1] *Abraham's vision* is to be found in Gn.15.12–17. *S.*
[2] *The Convex of Heaven*—Hell? *S.*

FRAGMENT B2

AT the end of double folio 3, the *Let* verses break off. Since they begin again later, we may assume that they were written but are lost. The *For* verses continue without a break through two double folios numbered by Smart "4" and "5", and these eight pages contain 475 lines which are here numbered 296–770 to indicate their continuity with the *For* verses of Fragment B1. This part of the poem appears to have been written between December 1759 and July or August 1760.

296 4. For the devil hath most power in winter, because darkness prevails.

For the Longing of Women is the operation of the Devil upon their conceptions.

For the marking of their children is from the same cause both of which are to be parried by prayer.

For the laws of King James ye first against Witchcraft were wise, had it been of man to make laws.

300 For there are witches and wizards even now who are spoken to by their familiars.[1]

For the visitation of their familiars is prevented by the Lord's incarnation.

For to conceive with intense diligence against one's neighbour is a branch of witchcraft.

For to use pollution, exact and cross things and at the same time to think against a man is the crime direct.

For prayer with musick is good for persons so exacted upon.[2]

305 For before the NATIVITY is the dead of the winter and after it the quick.

For the sin against the HOLY GHOST is INGRATITUDE.

For stuff'd guts make no musick; strain them strong and you shall have sweet melody.

For the SHADOW is of death,[3] which is the Devil, who can make false and faint images of the works of Almighty God.

For every man beareth death about him ever since the transgression of Adam, but in perfect light there is no shadow.

310 For all Wrath is Fire, which the adversary blows upon and exasperates.

For SHADOW is a fair Word from God, which is not returnable till the furnace comes up.[4]

---

[1] Smart's interest in witches and witchcraft is another link connecting him with the Cambridge Platonists. *S.*

[2] *Prayer with music:* "It seems the divell does not love Musick; but I know nothing else but does," Thomas Powell, *Human Industry* (1661), p. 120. *S.*

[3] *The Shadow is of death*, a repetition of B1.286.

[4] *The furnace comes up*, an echo of Abraham's vision, B1.293.

FRAGMENT B2

For the ECLIPSE [1] is of the adversary—blessed be the name of Jesus for Whisson of Trinity.

For the shadow is his and the penumbra is his and his the perplexity of the phenomenon.

For the eclipses happen at times when the light is defective.

315 For the more the light is defective, the more the powers of darkness prevail.

For deficiencies happen by the luminaries crossing one another.

For the SUN is an intelligence and an angel of the human form.

For the MOON is an intelligence and an angel in shape like a woman. [2]

For they are together in the spirit every night like man and wife.

320 For Justice is infinitely beneath Mercy in nature and office.

For the Devil himself may be just in accusation and punishment.

For HELL is without eternity from the presence of Almighty God.

For Volcanos & burning mountains are where the adversary hath most power.

For the angel GRATITUDE is my wife—God bring me to her or her to me.

325 For the propagation of light is quick as the divine Conception.

For FROST is damp & unwholsome air candied to fall to the best advantage.

For I am the Lord's News-Writer—the scribe-evangelist—Widow Mitchel, Gun & Grange bless the Lord Jesus.

For Adversity above all other is to be deserted of the grace of God.

For in the divine Idea this Eternity is compleat & the Word is a making many more.

---

[1] *Eclipse:* there was much interest at this time in the approaching transit of Venus over the sun, predicted for 1761; letters about it were printed in the *Gentleman's Magazine*, 1758, pp. 367–368, and 1760, pp. 265–266.

[2] "The Sun and Moon are two Magicall principles, the One active, the other passive, this *Masculine*, that *Fœminine*," Eugenius Philalethes [*i.e.* Thomas Vaughan], *Anthroposophia Theomagica* (1650), p. 24. *S.*

330 For there is a forlorn hope ev'n for impenitent sinners because the furnace itself must be the crown of Eternity.

For my hope is beyond Eternity in the bosom of God my saviour.

For by the grace of God I am the Reviver of ADORATION amongst ENGLISH-MEN.

For being desert—ed [1] is to have desert in the sight of God and intitles one to the Lord's merit.

For things that are not in the sight of men are thro' God of infinite concern.

335 For envious men have exceeding subtlety quippe qui in—videant. [2]

For avaricious men are exceeding subtle like the soul seperated from the body.

For their attention is on a sinking object which perishes.

For they can go beyond the children of light in matters of their own misery.

For Snow is the dew candied and cherishes. [3]

340 For TIMES and SEASONS are the Lord's [4]—Man is no CHRONO-LOGER.

For there is a CIRCULATION of the SAP in all vegetables.

For SOOT is the dross of Fire.

For the CLAPPING of the hands is naught unless it be to the glory of God.

For God will descend in visible glory when men begin to applaud him.

345 For all STAGE-Playing is Hypocrisy [5] and the Devil is the master of their revels.

---

[1] *Desert-ed*, a kind of philological quibble in which Smart delighted; see his Latin pun in B2.335, and the ridiculous series beginning at B2.627.

[2] *Quippe qui in-videant*, because they see into things; a pun on *invideant*, they envy. *S*.

[3] *Snow . . . cherishes*: examples are given in Derham's *Physico-Theology*, p. 24, note.

[4] *For Times and Seasons are the Lord's*: an echo of Ac.1.7, and a concept recurring in B2.576.

[5] *All Stage-Playing is Hypocrisy* represents a complete reversal of position for the man who wrote a comedy at college and promoted Mother Midnight's Oratory. *S*. There is more in this vein in C68 and C93.

FRAGMENT B2

For the INNATATION [1] of corpuscles is solved by the Gold-beater's hammer—God be gracious to Christopher Peacock and to all my God-Children.

For the PRECESSION of the Equinoxes is improving nature—something being gained every where for the glory of God perpetually.

For the souls of the departed are embodied in clouds and purged by the Sun.

For the LONGITUDE may be discovered by attending the motions of the Sun. Way 2^d.[2]

350 For you must consider the Sun as dodging, which he does to parry observation.

For he must be taken with an Astrolabe, & considerd respecting the point he left.

For you must do this upon your knees and that will secure your point.

For I bless God that I dwell within the sound of Success,[3] and that it is well with ENGLAND this blessed day. NATIVITY of our LORD N.S. 1759./

For a Man is to be looked upon in that which he excells as on a prospect.

355 For there be twelve cardinal virtues [4]—three to the East Greatness, Valour, Piety.

For there be three to the West—Goodness, Purity & Sublimity.

For there be three to the North—Meditation, Happiness, Strength.

---

[1] *Innatation* is not in *N.E.D.*, but the word is obviously allied to *innatant*, swimming or floating in or upon some liquid.

[2] Another obscurely-defined method of determining the longitude; see also B1.169.

[3] *The sound of Success:* the year ended with various celebrations for the successes of British and allied arms during 1759, which had seen Minden and Quebec and Hawke's defeat of the French fleet at Quiberon Bay. Even if he were confined, Smart could scarcely have avoided hearing echoes of the public festivities. This line ends with a heavy slanting stroke, indicative of a break perhaps similar to that after B1.122.

[4] The twelve virtues reappear in the same order in B2.603–615, and again in the same order in *S.D.*, 19–21:

> "Great, valiant, pious, good, and clean,
> Sublime, contemplative, serene,
>   Strong, constant, pleasant, wise!"

For there be three to the South—Constancy, Pleasantry and Wisdom.

For the Argument A PRIORI is GOD in every man's CONSCIENCE.

360 For the Argument A POSTERIORI is God before every man's eyes.

For the Four and Twenty Elders [1] of the Revelation are Four and Twenty Eternities.

For their Four and Twenty Crowns are their respective Consummations.

For a CHARACTER is the votes of the Worldlings, but the seal is of Almighty GOD alone.

For there is no musick in flats & sharps which are not in God's natural key. [2]

365 For where Accusation takes the place of encouragement a man of Genius is driven to act the vices of a fool.

For the Devil can set a house on fire, when the inhabitants find combustibles.

For the old account of time is the true [3]—Decr 28th 1759–60 ——

For Faith as a grain of mustard seed [4] is to believe, as I do, that an Eternity is such in respect to the power and magnitude of Almighty God.

For a DREAM is a good thing from GOD. [5]

370 For there is a dream from the adversary which is terror.

For the phenomenon of dreaming is not of one solution, but many.

For Eternity is like a grain of mustard as a growing body & improving spirit.

For the malignancy of fire is oweing to the Devil's hiding of light, till it became visible darkness. [6]

For the Circle may be SQUARED by swelling and flattening.

---

[1] *The Four and Twenty Elders* appear with their golden crowns in Rev.4.4. *S*.

[2] *God's natural key* probably reflects Smart's attitude towards contemporary experiments with the tempered scale, not firmly established in England until much later. Here, as in the matter of calendar reform (B2.367), Smart instinctively resisted change.

[3] The change of the calendar from Old to New Style had taken place in 1752.

[4] See also B2.372.

[5] *For a Dream is a good thing from God*, a phrase from Homer. *S*.

[6] *Visible darkness* is an echo from *Paradise Lost*, I, 63. *S*.

FRAGMENT B2

375 For the Life of God is in the body of man and his spirit in the Soul.

For there was no rain in Paradise because of the delicate construction of the spiritual herbs and flowers.

For the Planet Mercury is the WORD DISCERNMENT.[1]

For the Scotchman seeks for truth at the bottom of a well, the Englishman in the Heavn of Heavens.[2]

For the Planet Venus is the WORD PRUDENCE or providence.

380 For GOD nevertheless is an extravagant BEING and generous unto loss.

For there is no profit in the generation of man and the loss of millions is not worth God's tear.

For is the twelfth day of the MILLENNIUM of the MILLENNIUM foretold by the prophets give the glory to God ONE THOUSAND SEVEN HUNDRED AND SIXTY——

For the Planet Mars is the word FORTITUDE.

For to worship naked in the Rain is the bravest thing for the refreshing & purifying the body.

385 For the Planet Jupiter is the WORD DISPENSATION.

For Tully says to be generous you must be first just, but the voice of Christ is distribute at all events.

For Kittim is the father of the Pygmies,[3] God be gracious to Pigg his family.

For the Soul is divisible & a portion of the Spirit may be cut off from one & applied to another.

---

[1] Smart's planetary attributes agree closely with those given by the astrologers, among whom Mercury is the Intellect (hence Discernment), Venus is the Virgin (Prudence), Mars is War (Fortitude), Jupiter dispenses Justice (Dispensation), and Saturn is Chronos, Time, Tempus, the old god (Temperance or Patience). *S.* Smart's first Tripos poem, "Datur mundorum pluralitas" (or, in Francis Fawkes's translation, "A Voyage to the Planets," *Poems* (1752), pp. 138–151), dealt in broadly satirical vein with the attributes of the planets.

[2] *The Scotchman seeks for truth at the bottom of a well* is perhaps a contrast of Hume with Newton (*S.*) or with Derham.

[3] *Kittim* as ancestor of the Pygmies appears to be Smart's own invention. *S.*

JUBILATE AGNO

For NEW BREAD is the most wholesome especially if it be leaven'd with honey.[1]

390 For a NEW SONG also is best, if it be to the glory of God; & taken with the food like the psalms.

For the Planet Saturn is the word TEMPERANCE or PATIENCE.

For Jacob's Ladder are the steps of the Earth graduated hence to Paradice and thence to the throne of God.[2]

For a good wish is well but a faithful prayer is an eternal benefit.

For SPICA VIRGINIS is the star that appeared to the wise men in the East and directed their way before it was yet insphered.

395 For an IDEA is the mental vision of an object.

For Locke supposes that an human creature, at a given time may be an atheist i.e. without God, by the folly of his doctrine concerning innate ideas.[3]

For it is not lawful to sell poyson in England any more than it is in Venice, the Lord restrain both the finder and receiver.

For the ACCENTS are the invention of the Moabites, who learning the GREEK tongue marked the words after their own vicious pronuntiation.[4]

For the GAULS (the now-French and original Moabites) after they were subdued by Cæsar became such Grecians at Rome.

400 For the Gaullic manuscripts fell into the hands of the inventors of printing.[5]

---

[1] Partly repeated in B2.463.

[2] *Jacob's Ladder* as the steps to Paradise was a familiar image of the Cambridge Platonists. *S*.

[3] Smart argues that Locke, by denying the existence of innate ideas, implies that we all begin as atheists; but that, of course, is not fair to Locke, who opposed the materialism of Hobbes and sought to demonstrate the existence of God as necessary to knowledge and being. Locke's *Essay* is one of Smart's recorded borrowings from Pembroke College Library. *S*.

[4] The *accents* were introduced by Alexandrian scholars and systematized by Aristophanes of Byzantium, librarian at Alexandria about 195 B.C. *S*.

[5] *The inventors of printing* did, in fact, form their work quite frankly in imitation of the manuscripts currently in circulation. Smart's mind reverts to the technique of printing four lines later.

FRAGMENT B2

For all the inventions of man, which are good, are the communications of Almighty God.

For all the stars have satellites, which are terms under their respective words.

For tiger is a word and his satellites are Griffin, Storgis, Cat and others.

For my talent is to give an impression upon words by punching, that when the reader casts his eye upon 'em, he takes up the image from the mould wch I have made.[1]

405 For JOB was the son of Issachar [2] and patience is the child of strength.

For the Names of the DAYS, as they now stand, are foolish & abominable.[3]

For the Days are the First, Second, Third, Fourth, Fifth, Sixth and Seventh.

For the names of the months are false—the Hebrew appellatives are of God.

For the Time of the Lord's temptation was in early youth and imminent danger.

410 For an equivocal generation [4] is a generation and no generation.

For putrifying matter nevertheless will yeild up its life in diverse creatures and combinations of creatures.

---

[1] *My talent is to give an impression upon words:* a theory later expanded in Smart's introduction to his verse-translation of Horace (1767), I, xii: "*Impression* then, is a talent or gift of Almighty God, by which a Genius is impowered to throw an emphasis upon a word or sentence in such wise, that it cannot escape any reader of sheer good sense, and true critical sagacity." (Cited by Stead.) Smart's estimate of his own powers is revealed by comparing these passages. The imagery of the statement in *Jubilate* derives from the process of type-founding, in which a matrix receives the impression of a punch and is then placed in a mould to cast letters.

[2] *Job [who] was the son of Issachar,* Gn.46.13, is not the same as the Job of legendary patience; the identity of name led Smart astray.

[3] Smart here expounds a view strongly held by the Quakers. *S.*

[4] *Equivocal generation* is the same as spontaneous or anomalous generation; Derham, *Physico-Theology*, p. 413, n. 1: "The Doctrine of Æquivocal Generation, is at this Day so sufficiently exploded by all Learned Philosophers, that I shall not enter into the Dispute, but take it for granted, that all Animals spring from other Parent-Animals." Here, as elsewhere, Smart seems to be aware of the most enlightened views then current, and yet to be reluctant to abandon earlier error, as the next line shows.

For a TOAD can dwell in the centre of a stone,[1] because—there are stones whose constituent life is of those creatures.

For a Toad hath by means of his eye the most beautiful prospects of any other animal to make him amends for his distance from his Creator in Glory.

For FAT is the fruit of benevolence, therefore it was the Lord's in the Mosaic sacrifices.

415 For the very particular laws of Moses are the determinations of CASES that fell under his cognizance.

For the Devil can make the shadow thicker by candlelight by reason of his powr over malignant fire.

For the Romans clipped their words in the Augustan thro idleness and effeminacy and paid foreign actors for speaking them out.[2]

For when the weight and the powr are equivalent the prop is of none effect.

For shaving of the beard was an invention of the people of Sodom to make men look like women.[3]

420 For the ends of the world are the accomplishment of great events, and the consummation of periods.

For ignorance is a sin because illumination is to be obtained by prayer.[4]

For Preferment is not from the East, West or South, but from the North, where Satan has most power.[5]

For the ministers of the Devil set the hewer of wood over the head of God's free Man.

For this was inverting God's good order, edifice and edification, and appointing place, where the Lord has not appointed.

---

[1] It was still quite generally believed that toads could live in stones. The ideas in this and the next line are repeated in B2.580–583.

[2] *The Romans clipped their words:* the dandies minced their words and inserted or dropped the letter H. The Greek paidagogos was usual and often served as secretary or librarian. *S.* See also B2.579.

[3] Virtually repeated in B2.578.

[4] Virtually repeated in B2.570.

[5] *The North, where Satan has most power* again shows Smart's acquaintance with occult lore. *S.*

FRAGMENT B2

425 For the Ethiopian question is already solved in that the Blacks are the children of Cain.[1]

For the phenomenon of the horizontal moon is the truth—she appears bigger in the horizon because she actually is so.

For it was said of old 'can the Ethiopian change his skin?' the Lord has answered the question by his merit & death he shall.—

For the moon is magnified in the horizon by Almighty God, and so is the Sun.

For she has done her days-work and the blessing of God is upon her, and she communicates with the earth.

430 For when she rises she has been strengthned by the Sun, who cherishes her by night.

For man is born to trouble in the body, as the sparks fly upwards in the spirit.[2]

For man is between the pinchers while his soul is shaping and purifying.

For the ENGLISH are the seed of Abraham and work up to him by Joab, David, and Naphtali. God be gracious to us this day. General Fast March 14.th 1760.[3]

For the Romans and the English are one people the children of the brave man who died at the altar [4] praying for his posterity, whose death was the type of our Saviour's.

435 For the WELCH are the children of Mephibosheth and Ziba [5] with a mixture of David in the Jones's.

For the Scotch are the children of Doeg with a mixture of Cush the Benjamite, whence their innate antipathy to the English.

---

[1] *The Blacks are the children of Cain:* this and subsequent statements concerning the descent of modern races and nations from the tribes of Israel are by no means Smart's invention; Stead in a long note (p. 227) shows that they go back at least as far as Bede, and continue well into the nineteenth century.

[2] Almost a literal quotation of Job 5.7.

[3] *March 14th* 1760 was a day of public fasting and humiliation by royal proclamation; another indication of Smart's awareness of outside events even though confined. *S.*

[4] *The brave man who died at the altar* is probably Thomas Becket, already referred to sympathetically in B1.134.

[5] *Mephibosheth and Ziba* appear together in *S.D.* 83. *S.*

JUBILATE AGNO

For the IRISH are the children of Shimei and Cush with a mixture of something lower—the Lord raise them!

For the French are Moabites even the children of Lot.

For the DUTCH are the children of Gog.

440 For the Poles are the children of Magog.

For the Italians are the children of Samuel & are the same as the Grecians.

For the Spaniards are the children of Abishai Joab's brother, hence is the goodwill between the two nations.

For the Portuguese are the children of Ammon—God be gracious to Lisbon [1] and send good angels amongst them!

For the Hottentots are the children of Gog with a Black mixture.

445 For the Russians are the Children of Ishmael.

For the Turks are the children of Esaw, which is Edom.

For the Wallachians are the children of Huz. God be gracious to Elizabeth Hughes, as she was.

For the Germans are the children of the Philistins even the seed of Anak.

For the Prussians are the children of Goliah [2]—but the present, whom God bless this hour, is a Campbell of the seed of Phinees.

450 For the Hanoverians are Hittites of the seed of Uriah. God save the king. [3]

For the Hessians are Philistines with a mixture of Judah.

For the Saxons are Benjamites, men of great subtlety & Marshal Saxe [4] was direct from Benjamin.

---

[1] *God be gracious to Lisbon,* a reference to the earthquake of 1755. *S.* This also refers to the traditional friendship between England and Portugal, and echoes B1.5.

[2] The *Prussians* as children of Goliah probably contains a reference to the six-foot soldiers of Frederick the Great. *S.*

[3] *God save the King* cannot refer to the accession of George III, as Stead suggests; this part of the poem was composed in March or April, 1760, and George II died suddenly on 25 October 1760.

[4] *Marshal Saxe,* Maurice, comte de Saxe (1696–1750), a Saxon whose giant frame and brilliant military exploits won him great reputation. *S.*

FRAGMENT B2

For the Danes are of the children of Zabulon.

For the Venetians are the children of Mark and Romans.

455 For the Swiss are Philistins of a particular family. God be gracious to Jonathan Tyers [1] his family and to all the people at Vaux Hall.

For the Sardinians [2] are of the seed of David—The Lord forward the Reformation amongst the good seed first.—

For the Mogul's people are the children of Phut.

For the Old Greeks and the Italians are one people, which are blessed in the gift of Musick by reason of the song of Hannah and the care of Samuel with regard to divine melody.

For the Germans and the Dutch are the children of the Goths and Vandals who did a good in destruction of books written by heathen Free-Thinkers against God. [3]

460 For there are Americans of the children of Toi.

For the Laplanders are the children of Gomer.

For the Phenomena of the Diving Bell [4] are solved right in the schools.

For NEW BREAD is the most wholesome—God be gracious to Baker. [5]

For the English are the children of Joab, Captain of the host of Israel, [6] who was the greatest man in the world to GIVE and to ATCHIEVE.

465 For TEA is a blessed plant and of excellent virtue. God give the Physicians more skill and honesty!

For nutmeg is exceeding wholesome and cherishing, neither does it hurt the liver.

For The Lightning before death is God's illumination in the spirit for preparation [7] and for warning,

[1] *Jonathan Tyers*, for many years the proprietor of Vauxhall Gardens; see *D.N.B. S.*
[2] See also B1.67.
[3] A reference to the destruction of the library at Alexandria. *S.*
[4] *The Phenomena of the Diving Bell* are discussed at some length in *The Wonders of Nature and Art* (published by Smart's father-in-law, J. Newbery, 1750), II, 407–412. *S.*
[5] See B2.389.
[6] *Joab* is bidden to "worship the Lord God of Hosts" in A60.
[7] *Preparation*, the only time Smart uses this spelling of the word.

JUBILATE AGNO

For Lavender Cotton is exceeding good for the teeth. God be gracious to Windsmore.[1]

For the Fern is exceeding good & pleasant to rub the teeth.

470 For a strong preperation of Mandragora is good for the gout.

For the Bark [2] was a communication from God and is sovereign.

For the method of curing an ague by terror is exaction.

For Exaction is the most accursed of all things, because it brought the Lord to the cross, his betrayers & murderers being such from their exaction.

For an Ague is the terror of the body, when the blessing of God is withheld for a season.

475 For benevolence is the best remedy in the first place and the bark in the second.

For, when the nation is at war, it is better to abstain from the punishment of criminals especially, every act of human vengeance being a check to the grace of God.

For the letter ל which signifies GOD [3] by himself is on the fibre of some leaf in every Tree.

For ל is the grain of the human heart & on the network of the skin.

For ל is in the veins of all stones both precious and common.

480 For ל is upon every hair both of man and beast.

---

[1] *God be gracious to Windsmore*, repeated in C31.

[2] *The Bark* is probably quinine, the Peruvian bark, the subject of an address by Nicholas Munckley before the Royal Society in 1758. It is referred to again in B2.475. *S.*

[3] *The letter ל which signifies God.* Smart has rightly taken the Hebrew letter Lamed as the equivalent of the English letter L, but he then takes this as the equivalent of the Hebrew word 'el (actually a pun); 'el, but not Lamed, stands for God, as in Elohim and at the end of the names of the Archangels, Gabriel and Raphael. *S.* This definition of the Hebrew letter and the statement of its universality were implicit in Smart's earlier ode "On the Eternity of the Supreme Being," lines 2–5 (Callan, I, 223):

> ". . . . whose great Name
> Deep in the human heart, and every atom
> The Air, the Earth or azure Main contains,
> In undecypher'd characters is wrote."

FRAGMENT B2

For ל is in the grain of wood.

For ל is in the ore of all metals.

for ל is on the scales of all fish.

For ל is on the petals of all flowers. .

485 For ל is upon all shells.

For ל is in the constituent particles of air.

For ל is on the mite of the earth.

For ל is in the water yea in every drop.

For ל is in the incomprehensible ingredients of fire.

490 For ל is in the stars the sun and in the Moon.

For ל is upon the Sapphire Vault.

For the doubling of flowers is the improvement of the gardners talent.[1]

For the flowers are great blessings.

For the Lord made a Nosegay in the medow with his disciples & preached upon the lily.[2]

495 For the angels of God took it out of his hand and carried it to the Height.

For a man cannot have publick spirit, who is void of private benevolence.

For there is no Height in which there are not flowers.

For flowers have great virtues for all the senses.

For the flower glorifies God and the root parries the adversary.

500 For the flowers have their angels even the words of God's Creation.

For the warp & woof of flowers are worked by perpetual moving spirits.

For flowers are good both for the living and the dead.

---

[1] The beautiful passage which follows suggests that Smart was a gardener, which is confirmed by Dr. Johnson's remark, "He digs in the garden," and by Smart's prayer elsewhere, "The Lord succeed my pink borders" (D118). *S*.

[2] *The Lord made a nosegay . . . with his disciples;* Smart is probably interpreting, or amplifying, the Greek text of Mk.6.40, where the meaning of πρασιαί is that the disciples sat down in groups like beds of herbs. But this is the Feeding of the Five Thousand, while "Consider the lilies" occurs in the Sermon on the Mount. *S*.

For there is a language of flowers.

For there is a sound reasoning upon all flowers.

505 For elegant phrases are nothing but flowers.

For flowers are peculiarly the poetry of Christ.

For flowers are medicinal.

For flowers are musical in ocular harmony.

For the right names of flowers are yet in heaven. God make gardners better nomenclators.

510 For the Poorman's nosegay is an introduction to a Prince.

For it were better for the SERVICE, if only select psalms were read.[1]

For the Lamentations of Jeremiah, Songs from other scriptures, and parts of Esdras might be taken to supply the quantity.

5. For A is the beginning of learning and the door of heaven.[2]

For B is a creature busy and bustling.

515 For C is a sense quick and penetrating.

For D is depth.

For E is eternity—such is the power of the English letters taken singly.

For F is faith.

For G is God—whom I pray to be gracious to Livemore my fellow prisoner.[3]

520 For H is not a letter, but a spirit—Benedicatur Jesus Christus, sic spirem!

For I is identity. God be gracious to Henry Hatsell.

---

[1] Smart returns to his scheme for reforming the Anglican liturgy, first noticed in B1.252, which led him to compose his metrical version of the Psalms (published 1765).

[2] The explanation of Smart's zeal in giving a meaning to the letters of the English alphabet is suggested in B2.517, "such is the power of the English letters taken singly"; he was familiar with the profound meanings attached to the Hebrew characters by occult writers, and evidently was trying to establish the significance of his native alphabet. *S.* He tries the exercise twice more in the surviving portions of the MS., at B2.538 and C1.

[3] *Livemore my fellow prisoner* is probably Ezra Livemore or Levermore, confined in Bethlehem and St. Luke's at various periods between 1758 and 1783. *S.*

FRAGMENT B2

For K is king.

For L is love. God in every language.

For M is musick and Hebrew מ is the direct figure of God's harp.[1]

525 For N is new.

For O is open.

For P is power.

For Q is quick.

For R is right.

530 For S is soul.

For T is truth. God be gracious to Jermyn Pratt and to Harriote his Sister.[2]

For U is unity, and his right name is Uve to work it double.

For W is word.

For X is hope—consisting of two check G—God be gracious to Anne Hope.[3]

535 For Y is yea. God be gracious to Bennet and his family![4]

For Z is zeal.

For in the education of children it is necessary to watch the words, which they pronounce with difficulty,[5] for such are against them in their consequences.

For A is awe, if pronounced full. Stand in awe and sin not.[6]

For B pronounced in the animal is bey importing authority.

---

[1] The Hebrew character is Mem, a symbol for waters; its resemblance to God's harp is apparently Smart's own idea derived from its appearance. *S.*

[2] *Jermyn Pratt* was Smart's contemporary at Cambridge, and his sister *Harriote* was one of Smart's former sweethearts, whom he addressed in five surviving poems (Callan, I, 187–191, 203) and renounced in a sixth (I, 202).

[3] *Anne Hope* was Smart's earliest sweetheart, and most tenderly remembered: see D186. *S.*

[4] *Bennet and his family*, probably an oblique reference to Miss Kitty Bennet, another girl to whom Smart once addressed a poem (Callan, I, 197). *S.*

[5] *The words which they pronounce with difficulty:* Smart was probably thinking of the fate of those who could not pronounce *Shibboleth*, Jg.12.6.

[6] *Stand in awe and sin not*, Ps.4.4. *S.*

540 For C pronounced hard is ke importing to shut.

For D pronounced full is day.

For E is east particularly when formed little e with his eye.

For F in its secondary meaning is fair.

For G in a secondary sense is good.

545 For H is heave.

For I is the organ of vision.

For K is keep.

For L is light, and ל is the line of beauty.

For M is meet.

550 For N is nay.

For O is over.

For P is peace.

For Q is quarter.

For R is rain, or thus reign, or thus rein.

555 For S is save.

For T is take.

For V is veil.

For W is world.

For X beginneth not, but connects and continues.

560 For Y is young—the Lord direct me in the better way going on in the Fifth year of my jeopardy June ye 17th N.S. 1760.[1] God be gracious to Dr YOUNG.

For Z is zest. God give us all a relish of our duty.

For Action & Speaking are one according to God and the Ancients.

For the approaches of Death are by illumination.

---

[1] *June ye 17th N.S.* 1760 is a very important date, as by *jeopardy* Smart meant his confinement (see B1.1), which he thus dates from 1756.

FRAGMENT B2

For a man cannot have Publick Spirit, who is void of private benevolence.

565 For the order of Alamoth is first three, second six, third eighteen, fourth fifty four, and then the whole band.

For the order of Sheminith [1] is first ten, second twenty, third thirty & then the whole band.

For the first entrance into Heaven is by complement.

For Flowers can see, and Pope's Carnations knew him. [2]

For the devil works upon damps and lowth [3] and causes agues.

570 For Ignorance is a sin, because illumination is to be had by prayer. [4]

For many a genius being lost at the plough is a false thought the divine providence is a better manager. [5]

For a man's idleness is the fruit of the adversary's diligence.

For diligence is the gift of God, as well as other good things.

For it is a good NOTHING in one's own eyes and in the eyes of fools.

575 For æra in its primitive sense is but a weed amongst corn. [6]

For there is no knowing of times & seasons, in submitting them to God stands the Christian's Chronology. [7]

For Jacob's brown sheep wore the Golden fleece.

For Shaving of the face was the invention of the Sodomites to make men look like women. [8]

---

[1] What Smart understood by *Alamoth* and *Sheminith* (which appear as directions in the headings of Ps. 46, 6, and 12) is not clear, especially as the Biblical interpretation of these terms has never really been settled. The former means literally "the maidens," the latter "the eighth." It is generally supposed that one refers to soprano voices, the other to bass; there seems to be no sanction for Smart's mathematical interpretation.

[2] Pope has a passage on the carnation, *Dunciad*, IV, 418 (*S.*), but it does not imply that the flowers "knew" him.

[3] *Lowth*, lowness or low-lying land.

[4] See B2.421.

[5] Here Smart is evidently taking issue with the sentiments of Gray's *Elegy* (1752). *S.*

[6] Among other meanings, *æra* is darnel, a weed-grass found in grainfields. *S.*

[7] See B2.340.

[8] See B2.419.

For God has given us a language of monosyllables to prevent our clipping.[1]

580 For a toad enjoys a finer prospect than another creature to compensate his lack.[2]

    Tho' toad I am the object of man's hate
    Yet better am I than a reprobate.   who has the worst of prospects.

For there are stones, whose constituent particles are little toads.

For the spiritual musick is as follows.[3]

585 For there is the thunder-stop, which is the voice of God direct.

For the rest of the stops are by their rhimes.

For the trumpet rhimes are sound bound, soar more and the like.

For the Shawm rhimes are lawn fawn moon boon and the like.

For the harp rhimes are sing ring, string & the like.

590 For the cymbal rhimes are bell well toll soul & the like.

For the flute rhimes are tooth youth suit mute & the like.

For the dulcimer rhimes are grace place beat heat & the like.

For the Clarinet rhimes are clean seen and the like.

For the Bassoon rhimes are pass, class and the like. ~~God be gracious to Baumgarden~~.

595 For the dulcimer are rather van fan & the like and grace place &c are of the bassoon.

For beat heat, weep peep &c are of the pipe.

For every word has its marrow in the English tongue for order and for delight.

---

[1] See B2.417.
[2] See B2.412–413.
[3] As Stead points out, the passage beginning here is important for an understanding of the rhythms and sonorities of *A Song to David*, which must have been forming in Smart's mind at this time: see the passage on the Virtues immediately following, which plays an important part in the *Song*. Smart had evidently given much thought to the sound-value of words, even though he expresses some of it rather naïvely. The closing lines of this passage read like a somewhat obscure statement of some of Robert Lowth's theories in *De sacra poesi Hebraeorum* (1753), as practised by Smart himself in this poem.

FRAGMENT B2

For the dissyllables such as able table &c are the fiddle rhimes.

For all dissyllables and some trissyllables are fiddle rhimes.

600 For the relations of words are in pairs first.

For the relations of words are sometimes in oppositions.

For the relations of words are according to their distances from the pair.

For there be twelve cardinal virtues the gifts of the twelve sons of Jacob.[1]

For Reuben is Great. God be gracious to Lord Falmouth.

605 For Simeon is Valiant. God be gracious to the Duke of Somerset.

For Levi is Pious. God be gracious to the Bishop of London.

For Judah is Good.[2] God be gracious to Lord Granville.

For Dan is Clean—neat, dextrous, apt, active, compact. God be gracious to Draper.

For Naphtali is sublime—God be gracious to Chesterfield.

610 For Gad is Contemplative—God be gracious to Lord Northampton.

For Ashur [3] is Happy—God be gracious to George Bowes.

For Issachar is strong—God be gracious to the Duke of Dorsett.

For Zabulon [4] is Constant—God be gracious to Lord Bath.

For Joseph is Pleasant—God be gracious to Lord Bolingbroke.

---

[1] The twelve sons of Jacob are named in order, and their association with the twelve virtues is not altogether arbitrary: thus *Asher* means *happy*, and *Issachar* is associated with *strength* in Gn.49.14. It is possible, as Brittain holds (pp. 298–299), that Smart was able to justify to himself the entire series of pairs, on the basis of Gn.30 and 49 and other scriptural passages. The difficulty here is that he must then have had these associations in mind a good deal earlier, when he first named the virtues in this order, B2.355–358. The associations with Smart's contemporaries certainly seem arbitrary, and in some cases downright inappropriate. For example, William Pulteney, 10th Earl of Bath, was reputed to be anything but constant; see *The Complete Peerage*, ed. Vicary Gibbs, II (1912), 23, note (b).

[2] *For Judah is good* is carried over into *S.D.*, 43, as "Good—from Jehudah's genuine vein."

[3] The eighth son of Jacob is properly *Asher*; the spelling *Ashur* occurs only in 1 Ch.2.24 and 4.5, and there evidently by mistake or corruption of the text. Smart uses the correct spelling in B1.41.

[4] *Zabulon* is the N.T. spelling of O.T. Zebulun.

III

615 For Benjamin is Wise—God be gracious to Honeywood.

For all Foundation is from God depending.

For the two Universities are the Eyes of England.

For Cambridge is the right and the brightest.

For Pembroke Hall was founded more in the Lord than any College in Cambridge.

620 For mustard is the proper food of birds & men are bound to cultivate it for their use.

For they that study the works of God are peculiarly assisted by his Spirit.

For all the creatures mentiond by Pliny are somewhere or other extant to the glory of God.

For Rye is food rather for fowls than men.

For Rye-bread is not taken with thankfulness.

625 For the lack of Rye may be supplied by Spelt.

For languages work into one another by their bearings.

For the power of some animal is predominant in every language.

For the power and spirit of a CAT is in the Greek.

For the sound of a cat is in the most useful preposition $κατ$' $ευχην$.[1]

630 For the pleasantry of a cat at pranks is in the language ten thousand times over.

For JACK UPON PRANCK is in the performance of $περι$ [2] together or seperate.

For Clapperclaw is in the grappling of the words upon one another in all the modes of versification.

For the sleekness of a Cat is in his $αγλαιηφι$.[3]

---

[1] This and the succeeding lines show once again Smart's preoccupation with the sound of language. They must not be taken as an indication of philological ignorance, for Smart was an accomplished classical scholar. The Greek phrase here is the equivalent of Latin *ex voto*, according to one's prayer, or by reason of a vow. *S.*

[2] $Περι$, around, concerning, near. *S.*

[3] $Αγλαιηφι$ (Ep. dat.), splendour, beauty, adornment, used of Penelope's appearance, *Od.* 18.180. *S.*

FRAGMENT B2

For the Greek is thrown from heaven and falls upon its feet.

635 For the Greek when distracted from the line is sooner restored to rank & rallied into some form than any other.

For the purring of a Cat is his $\tau\varrho v\zeta\epsilon\iota$.[1]

For his cry is in $ov\alpha\iota$,[2] which I am sorry for.

For the Mouse (Mus) prevails in the Latin.

For Edi-mus, bibi-mus, vivi-mus—ore-mus.[3]

640 For the Mouse is a creature of great personal valour.

For—this is a true case—Cat takes female mouse/from the company of male—male mouse will not depart, but stands threatning & daring.

For this is as much as to challenge, if you will let her go, I will engage you, as prodigious a creature as you are.

For the Mouse is of an hospitable disposition.

For bravery & hospitality were said & done by the Romans rather than others.

645 For two creatures the Bull & the Dog prevail in the English.

For all the words ending in ble are in the creature. Invisi-ble, Incomprehensi-ble, ineffa-ble, A-ble.

For the Greek & Latin are not dead languages, but taken up & accepted for the sake of him that spake them.

For can is (canis) is cause & effect a dog.

For the English is concise & strong. Dog & Bull again.

650 For Newton's notion of colours is $\alpha\lambda o\gamma o\varsigma$ unphilosophical.[4]

For the colours are spiritual.

For WHITE is the first and the best.

For there are many intermediate colours before you come to SILVER.

---

[1] $T\varrho v\zeta\epsilon\iota$; $\tau\varrho v\zeta\omega$ is used of the croaking of a frog; used of men, it means to mutter, to murmur. S.

[2] $Ov\alpha\iota$, the Greek for "Ah!" or "Woe!" S.

[3] For we eat, we drink we live—let us pray. S.

[4] The reference is to Sir Isaac Newton's *Opticks* (1704). S.

For the next colour is a lively GREY.

655 For the next colour is BLUE.

For the next is GREEN of which there are ten thousand distinct sorts.

For the next is YELLOW wch is more excellent than red, tho Newton makes red the prime. God be gracious to John Delap.

For RED is the next working round the Orange.

For Red is of sundry sorts till it deepens to BLACK.

660 For black blooms and it is PURPLE.

For purple works off to BROWN which is of ten thousand acceptable shades.

For the next is PALE. God be gracious to William Whitehead.

For pale works about to White again.

NOW that colour is spiritual appears inasmuch as the blessing of God upon all things descends in colour.

665 For the blessing of health upon the human face is in colour.

For the blessing of God upon purity is in the Virgin's blushes.

For the blessing of God in colour is on him that keeps his virgin.

For I saw a blush in Staindrop Church,[1] which was of God's own colouring.

For it was the benevolence of a virgin shewn to me before the whole congregation.

670 For the blessing of God upon the grass is in shades of Green visible to a nice observer as they light upon the surface of the earth.

For the blessing of God unto perfection in all bloom & fruit is by colouring.

For from hence something in the spirit may be taken off by painters.

For Painting is a species of idolatry, tho' not so gross as statuary.

For it is not good to look with earning [2] upon any dead work.

---

[1] *A blush in Staindrop Church* (which is adjacent to Raby Castle) is once more a reminiscence of Smart's lost love, Anne Hope. *S.*

[2] *With earning*, see note on B1.165.

FRAGMENT B2

675   For by so doing something is lost in the spirit & given from life to death.

For BULL in the first place is the word of Almighty God.[1]

For he is a creature of infinite magnitude in the height.

For there is the model of every beast of the field in the height.

For they are blessed intelligences & all angels of the living God.

680   For there are many words under Bull.

For Bul the Month is under it.

For Sea is under Bull.

For Brook is under Bull. God be gracious to Lord Bolingbroke.

For Rock is under Bull.

685   For Bullfinch is under Bull. God be gracious to the Duke of Cleveland.

For God, which always keeps his work in view has painted a Bullfinch in the heart of a stone. God be gracious to Gosling and Canterbury.

For the Bluecap is under Bull.

For the Humming Bird is under Bull.

For Beetle is under Bull.

690   For Toad is under bull.

For Frog is under Bull, which he has a delight to look at.

For the Pheasant-eyed Pink is under Bull. Blessed Jesus RANK EL.[2]

For Bugloss is under Bull.

For Bugle is under Bull.

695   For Oxeye is under Bull.

For Fire is under Bull.

For I will consider my Cat Jeoffry.

For he is the servant of the Living God duly and daily serving him.

---

[1] At least a part of this concept of the *Bull* derives from Cabbalistic thought. *S.*
[2] *Rank El* is unexplained.

For at the first glance of the glory of God in the East he worships in his way.

700 For is this done by wreathing his body seven times round with elegant quickness.

For then he leaps up to catch the musk, wch is the blessing of God upon his prayer.

For he rolls upon prank to work it in.

For having done duty and received blessing he begins to consider himself.

For this he performs in ten degrees.

705 For first he looks upon his fore-paws to see if they are clean.

For secondly he kicks up behind to clear away there.

For thirdly he works it upon stretch with the fore paws extended.

For fourthly he sharpens his paws by wood.

For fifthly he washes himself.

710 For Sixthly he rolls upon wash.

For Seventhly he fleas himself, that he may not be interrupted upon the beat.[1]

For Eighthly he rubs himself against a post.

For Ninthly he looks up for his instructions.

For Tenthly he goes in quest of food.

715 For having consider'd God and himself he will consider his neighbour.

For if he meets another cat he will kiss her in kindness.

For when he takes his prey he plays with it to give it a chance.

For one mouse in seven escapes by his dallying.

For when his day's work is done his business more properly begins.

720 For he keeps the Lord's watch in the night against the adversary.

For he counteracts the powers of darkness by his electrical skin & glaring eyes.

---

[1] *That he may not be interrupted upon the beat,* so that he will not have to interrupt his activities (by scratching).

116

For he counteracts the Devil, who is death, by brisking about the life.

For in his morning orisons he loves the sun and the sun loves him.

For he is of the tribe of Tiger.

725 For the Cherub Cat is a term of the Angel Tiger.

For he has the subtlety and hissing of a serpent, which in goodness he suppresses.

For he will not do destruction if he is well-fed, neither will he spit without provocation.

For he purrs in thankfulness, when God tells him he's a good Cat.

For he is an instrument for the children to learn benevolence upon.

730 For every house is incompleat without him & a blessing is lacking in the spirit.

For the Lord commanded Moses concerning the cats at the departure of the Children of Israel from Egypt.[1]

For every family had one cat at least in the bag.

For the English Cats are the best in Europe.

For he is the cleanest in the use of his fore-paws of any quadrupede.

735 For the dexterity of his defence is an instance of the love of God to him exceedingly.

For he is the quickest to his mark of any creature.

For he is tenacious of his point.

For he is a mixture of gravity and waggery.

For he knows that God is his Saviour.

740 For there is nothing sweeter than his peace when at rest.

For there is nothing brisker than his life when in motion.

For he is of the Lord's poor and so indeed is he called by benevolence perpetually—Poor Jeoffry! poor Jeoffry! the rat has bit thy throat.

For I bless the name of the Lord Jesus that Jeoffry is better.

[1] The *cat* does not appear in the Bible.

JUBILATE AGNO

For the divine spirit comes about his body to sustain it in compleat cat

745 For his tongue is exceeding pure so that it has in purity what it wants in musick.

For he is docile and can learn certain things.

For he can set up with gravity which is patience upon approbation.

For he can fetch and carry, which is patience in employment.

For he can jump over a stick which is patience upon proof positive.

750 For he can spraggle upon waggle at the word of command.

For he can jump from an eminence into his master's bosom.

For he can catch the cork and toss it again.

For he is hated by the hypocrite and miser.

For the former is affraid of detection.

755 For the latter refuses the charge.

For he camels his back to bear the first notion of business.

For he is good to think on, if a man would express himself neatly.

For he made a great figure in Egypt for his signal services.

For he killed the Icneumon-rat very pernicious by land.[1]

760 For his ears are so acute that they sting again.

For from this proceeds the passing quickness of his attention.

For by stroaking of him I have found out electricity.

For I perceived God's light about him both wax and fire.

For the Electrical fire is the spiritual substance, which God sends from heaven to sustain the bodies both of man and beast.

765 For God has blessed him in the variety of his movements.

For, tho he cannot fly, he is an excellent clamberer.

[1] Smart had an erroneous conception of the *Ichneumon*, which is regarded as beneficial, not pernicious, and which destroys rats and mice. *S.*

118

FRAGMENT B2

For his motions upon the face of the earth are more than any other quadrupede.

For he can tread to all the measures upon the musick.

For he can swim for life.

770 For he can creep.

FRAGMENT C

A LONG hiatus follows Fragment B2, which ends with double folio 5. The next surviving double folio is numbered "10" and is the beginning of the *Let* verses of Fragment D. Somewhere in this gap falls the pair of unnumbered single leaves of *Let* and *For* verses, each containing 162 lines and here printed *vis-à-vis* in the manner of Fragment B1. These leaves show a torn edge on the left-hand side, and it seems safe to assume that they are the second leaves of what were originally double folios. The dates in the text range from March to May 1761, so they were probably either numbered "7" or "8". The dates also indicate a steady rate of composition of two pairs of lines per day.

JUBILATE AGNO

Let Ramah [1] rejoice with Cochineal.

Let Gaba rejoice with the Prickly Pear, which the Cochineal feeds on.

Let Nebo rejoice with the Myrtle-Leaved-Sumach as with the Skirrel Jub. 2^{d}.[2]

Let Magbish rejoice with the Sage-Tree Phlomis as with the Goatsbeard Jub: 2^{d}.

5 Let Hashum rejoice with Moon-Trefoil.

Let Netophah rejoice with Cow-Wheat.

Let Chephirah rejoice with Millet.

Let Beeroth rejoice with Sea-Buckthorn.

Let Kirjath-arim rejoice with Cacalianthemum. [3]

10 Let Hadid rejoice with Capsicum Guiney Pepper.

Let Senaah rejoice with Bean Cape.

Let Kadmiel rejoice with Hemp-Agrimony.

Let Shobai rejoice with Arbor Molle.

Let Hatita rejoice with Millefolium Yarrow.

15 Let Ziha rejoice with Mitellia.

Let Hasupha rejoice with Turky Balm.

Let Hattil rejoice with Xeranthemum.

---

[1] Most of the Biblical names in this section are to be found in the books of Ezra and Nehemiah, and it is perhaps indicative of Smart's changed attitude towards his original design that he uses place-names and personal-names quite indifferently. The names in 1–34 are all from Ezra 2. Smart seems to be much more interested in the herbs and flowers, and as Stead points out he agrees closely with the herbals of his day in assigning them attributes. There are some indications that he was familiar with Philip Miller's *The Gardener's Dictionary* (1731–1739).

[2] *Jub. 2d.* seems to mean *Jubilate 2d. S.* Perhaps Smart means that he has already coupled Nebo with Skirrel and Magbish with Goatsbeard in the (now missing) second double folio of the poem.

[3] *Cacalianthemum* is repeated in C99.

FRAGMENT C

For H is a spirit and therefore he is God.[1]

For I is person and therefore he is God.

For K is king and therefore he is God.

For L is love and therefore he is God.

5 For M is musick and therefore he is God.

For N is novelty and therefore he is God.

For O is over and therefore he is God.

For P is power and therefore he is God.

For Q is quick and therefore he is God.

10 For R is right and therefore he is God.

For S is soul and therefore he is God.

For T is truth and therefore he is God.

For U is union and therefore he is God.

For W is worth and therefore he is God.

15 For X has the pow'r of three [2] and therefore he is God.

For Y is yea and therefore he is God.

For Z is zeal and therefore he is God, whom I pray to be gracious to the Widow Davis and Davis the Bookseller.

---

[1] On Smart's exercises on the alphabet, see B2.513, note.
[2] The letter X is pronounced EKS and thus has the value of three letters; also it contains a V, an inverted V, and its own significance as X. *S.*

JUBILATE AGNO

18 Let Bilshan rejoice with the Leek. David for ever! God bless the Welch March 1ˢᵗ 1761. N. S.[1]

Let Sotai rejoice with the Mountain Ebony.

20 Let Sophereth rejoice with White Hellebore.

Let Darkon rejoice with the Melon-Thistle.

Let Jaalah rejoice with Moly wild garlick.

Let Ami rejoice with the Bladder Sena in season or out of season bless the name of the Lord.

Let Pochereth rejoice with Fleabane.

25 Let Keros rejoice with Tree Germander.

Let Padon rejoice with Tamnus Black Briony.

Let Mizpar rejoice with Stickadore.

Let Baanah rejoice with Napus the French Turnip.

Let Reelaiah rejoice with the Sea-Cabbage.

30 Let Parosh rejoice with Cacubalus Chickweed.

Let Hagab rejoice with Serpyllum Mother of Thyme. Hosanna to the memory of Q. Anne. March 8ᵗʰ N. S. 1761 [2]—God be gracious to old Windsmore.

Let Shalmai rejoice with Meadow Rue.

Let Habaiah rejoice with Asteriscus Yellow Starwort.

Let Tel-harsa rejoice with Aparine Clivers.

35 Let Rehoboam rejoice with Polium Montanum. God give grace to the Young King.[3]

---

[1] The *Leek* is chosen because of the date, March 1, St. David's Day; hence the exclamation, *God bless the Welsh*. S.

[2] March 8 is the anniversary of the accession of Queen Anne. The coincidence of date with verse 32 of the *For* section is the first real link between the two halves of this fragment.

[3] *Rehoboam* was the son and successor to Solomon, reminding Smart of George III whose reign had begun only a few months earlier, 25 October 1760.

FRAGMENT C

18 For Christ being A and Ω [1] is all the intermediate letters without doubt.

For there is a mystery in numbers. [2]

20 For One is perfect and good being at unity in himself.

For Two is the most imperfect of all numbers.

For every thing infinitely perfect is Three.

For the Devil is two being without God.

For he is an evil spirit male and female.

25 For he is called the Duce by foolish invocation on that account.

For Three is the simplest and best of all numbers.

For Four is good being square.

For Five is not so good in itself but works well in combination.

For Five is not so good in itself as it consists of two and three.

30 For Six is very good consisting of twice three.

For Seven is very good consisting of two compleat numbers.

For Eight is good for the same reason and propitious to me Eighth of March 1761 hallelujah.

For Nine is a number very good and harmonious.

For Cipher is a note of augmentation very good.

35 For innumerable ciphers will amount to something.

---

[1] *For Christ being A and Ω*, see Rev.1.8. *S.*

[2] *For there is a mystery in numbers* is another facet of Smart's exploration of the occult. Pembroke College Library records his borrowing of Iamblichus's *Life of Pythagoras*, and the following lines parallel at many points statements in Henry Cornelius Agrippa, *Three Books of Occult Philosophy* (1651). *S.*

JUBILATE AGNO

36 Let Hanan rejoice with Poley of Crete.

Let Sheshbazzar rejoice with Polygonatum Solomon's seal.

Let Zeboim rejoice with Bastard Dittany.

Let The Queen of Sheba rejoice with Bulapathon Herb Patience.

40 Let Cyrus rejoice with Baccharis Plowman's Spikenard. God be gracious to Warburton.

Let Lebanah rejoice with the Golden Wingged Flycatcher a Mexican Small Bird of Passage.

Let Hagabah rejoice with Orchis Blessed be the name of the Lord Jesus for my seed in eternity.[1]

Let Siaha rejoice with the Razor-Fish. God be gracious to John Bird [2] and his wife.

Let Artaxerxes rejoice with Vanelloes. Palm Sunday 1761.[3] The Lord Strengthen me.

45 Let Bishlam rejoice with the Cotton-bush.

Let Mithredath rejoice with Balsam of Tolu.

Let Tabeel rejoice with the Carob-Tree.

Let Ariel rejoice with Balsam of Peru, which sweats from a tree, that flowers like the Foxglove.

Let Ebed rejoice with Balsam of Gilead. God be gracious to Stede.

50 Let Jarib rejoice with Balsam of Capivi. The Lord strengthen my reins.

---

[1] *Orchis* has remarkable sexual powers according to Pliny, which Smart seems to have spiritualized in his phrase, *my seed in eternity. S. Hagabah* is so spelled in Ezra 2.45; the name reappears in C134 among a series deriving from Neh.7 as *Hagaba*, its spelling in Neh.7.48. Either Smart's memory for detail was truly remarkable, or he had a copy of the Bible at hand while working on these lines.

[2] *John Bird* (1709–1776), a famous maker of mathematical instruments. *S.* He may be the source of Smart's information about the problem of calculating the longitude, mentioned in B1.169, B1.190 and B2.349.

[3] *Palm Sunday 1761*, 15 March.

FRAGMENT C

36 For the mind of man cannot bear a tedious accumulation of nothings without effect.

For infinite upon infinite they make a chain.[1]

For the last link is from man very nothing ascending to the first Christ the Lord of All.

For the vowell is the female spirit in the Hebrew consonant.[2]

40 For there are more letters in all languages not communicated.

For there are some that have the power of sentences. O rare thirteenth of march 1761.

For St Paul was caught up into the third heavens.[3]

For there he heard certain words which it was not possible for him to understand.

For they were constructed by uncommunicated letters.

45 For they are signs of speech too precious to be communicated for ever.

For after ת there follows another letter in the Hebrew tongue.

For his name is Wau and his figure is thus ～�～.[4]

For the Æolians knew something of him in the spirit, but could not put him down.

For the figures were first communicated to Esau. God be gracious to Musgrave.

50 For he was blest as a merchant.

---

[1] The mathematical sign for infinity is ∞. *S.*

[2] The noun for vowel (ṫenuah) is feminine in Hebrew. *S.* This may represent another link between the *Let* and *For* verses.

[3] See 2 Cor.12.2–4. *S.*

[4] What Smart has written appears to be the last letter in the Hebrew alphabet; but as his reference is to the Hebrew tongue, he may mean that when *tau* is pronounced, *vau* is needed to complete the sound. This, however, leaves unexplained the curious figure with which he ends the line. *S.*

51 Let Shimshai rejoice with Stelis Missletoe on Fir.

Let Joiarib rejoice with Veronica Fluellen or Speedwell.

Let Tatnai rejoice with the Barbadoes Wild Olive.

Let Ezra rejoice with the Reed. The Lord Jesus make musick of it. Good Friday 1761.

55 Let Josiphiah rejoice with Tower-Mustard. God be gracious to Durham School.[1]

Let Shether-boznai rejoice with Turnera. End of Lent 1761. No. 5.[2]

Let Jozadak rejoice with Stephanitis a vine growing naturally into chaplets.

Let Jozabad rejoice with the Lily-Daffodil. Easter Day 22ᵈ March 1761.

Let Telem [3] rejoice with Hart's Penny-royal.

60 Let Abdi rejoice with Winter-green. God be gracious to Abdy.

Let Binnui rejoice with Spotted Lungwort or Couslip of Jerusalem. God give blessing with it.

Let Aziza rejoice with the Day Lily.

Let Zabbai rejoice with Buckshorn Plaintain Coronopus.

Let Ramoth rejoice with Persicaria.

---

[1] *Durham School*, Smart's school. *S.*

[2] *No. 5* is unexplained.

[3] *Telem* begins a series of names apparently derived from Ezra 10, continuing to line 89.

FRAGMENT C

51 For the blessing of Jacob was in the spirit and Esau's for temporal thrift.

For the story of Orpheus is of the truth.[1]

For there was such a person a cunning player on the harp.

For he was a believer in the true God and assisted in the spirit.

55 For he playd upon the harp in the spirit by breathing upon the strings.

For this will affect every thing that is sustaind by the spirit, even every thing in nature.

For it is the business of a man gifted in the word to prophecy good.

For it will .be better for England and all the world in a season, as I prophecy this day.

For I prophecy that they will obey the motions of the spirit descended upon them as at this day.

60 For they have seen the glory of God already come down upon the trees.[2]

For I prophecy that it will descend upon their heads also.

For I prophecy that the praise of God will be in every man's mouth in the Publick streets.[3]

For I prophecy that there will be Publick worship in the cross ways and fields.

For I prophecy that the general salutation will be. The Lord Jesus prosper you. I wish you good luck in the name of the Lord Jesus!

---

[1] An echo of Smart's earlier ode "On the Goodness of the Supreme Being," (Callan, I, 240):

> "Orpheus, for so the Gentiles call'd thy name,
> Israel's sweet psalmist. . . ."

Brittain has shown that Smart was following Patrick Delaney's *An Historical Account of the Life and Reign of David, King of Israel* (1740–1742) in identifying Orpheus with David. *S.*

[2] *The glory of God come down upon the trees* seems to be related to the doctrine of B2.664.

[3] Smart again refers to his habit of public prayer; see B1.89–90.

JUBILATE AGNO

65 Let Athlai rejoice with Bastard Marjoram.

Let Uel rejoice with Lysimachia Loose-strife which drinks of the brook by the way.

Let Kelaiah rejoice with Hermannia.

Let Elasah rejoice with Olibanum White or Male Frankinsense from an Arabian tree, good against Catarrhs and Spitting blood [1] from which Christ Jesus deliver me.

Let Adna [2] rejoice with Gum Opopanax from the wounded root of a species of panace Heracleum a tall plant growing to be two or three yards high with many large wings of a yellowish green—good for old coughs and asthmas.

70 Let Bedeiah rejoice with Gum Sagapenum flowing from a species of Ferula which grows in Media. Lord have mercy on my breast.

Let Ishijah rejoice with Sago gotten from the inward pith of the bread-tree. The Lord Jesus strengthen my whole body.

Let Chelal rejoice with Apios Virginian Liquorice Vetch.

Let Miamin rejoice with Mezereon. God be gracious to Polly and Bess and all Canbury. [3]

Let Zebina [4] rejoice with Tormentil good for hæmorrhages in the mouth even so Lord Jesus.

75 Let Shemaria rejoice with Riciasides.

Let Jadau rejoice with Flixweed.

Let Shimeon rejoice with Squills.

Let Sheal rejoice with Scorpioides. God be gracious to Legg.

Let Ramiah rejoice with Water-Germander.

---

[1] *Catarrhs and Spitting blood*, see B1.179, note. As Stead observes, the specifics mentioned are in accord with eighteenth-century medical practice.

[2] *Adna* means *pleasure*, making a possible link between *Let* and *For* verses.

[3] *Polly and Bess and all Canbury:* this looks as though Polly lived at Canonbury; see notes on B1.55 and B1.75. Bess was perhaps Smart's daughter Elizabeth Anne. *S.*

[4] Smart wrote *Zebida* (*Zebidah* occurs in 2 K.23.36) evidently by mistake; the present series of names comes from Ezra 10, where occurs the name *Zebina*, presumably what he intended. This evidence points in precisely the opposite direction to that cited in C42, note.

FRAGMENT C

65 For I prophecy that there will be more mercy for criminals.

For I prophecy that there will be less mischief concerning women.

For I prophecy that they will be cooped up and kept under due controul.

For I prophecy that there will be full churches and empty play-houses.[1]

For I prophecy that they will learn to take pleasure in glorifying God with great cheerfulness.

70 For I prophecy that they will observe the Rubrick with regard to days of Fasting & Abstinence.

For I prophecy that the clergy in particular will set a better example.

For I prophecy that they will not dare to imprison a brother or sister for debt.

For I prophecy that hospitality and temperance will revive.

For I prophecy that men will be much stronger in the body.

75 For I prophecy that the gout, and consumptions will be curable.

For I prophecy that man will be as good as a Lupine.

For the Lupine professes his Saviour in Grain.

For the very Hebrew letter is fairly graven upon his Seed.

For with diligence the whole Hebrew Alphabet may be found in a parcel of his seed.[2]

---

[1] An echo of an earlier statement at B2.345; see also C93.

[2] The Hebrew letters to be found on the seed of the Lupine represent an extension of the idea behind B2.477–491.

80 Let Jeziah rejoice with Viper's Grass.

Let Machnadebai rejoice with the Mink, a beast.

Let Meremoth rejoice with the Golden Titmouse of Surinam.

Let Mattenai rejoice with Hatchet Vetch.

Let Chelluh rejoice with Horehound.

85 Let Jaasau rejoice with Bird's foot.

Let Maadai rejoice with Golden Rod.

Let Sharai rejoice with Honey-flower.

Let Shashai rejoice with Smyrnium.

Let Hananiah the son of an apothecary rejoice with Bdellium.

90 Let Hassenaah rejoice with the White Beet. God be gracious to Hasse [1] and all musicians.

Let Hachaliah rejoice with Muscus Arboreus.

Let Sanballat rejoice with Ground Moss found sometimes on human skulls.

Let Col-hozeh [2] rejoice with Myrobalans, Bellerica, Chebula, Citrina, Emblica & Indica.

Let Meah rejoice with Variæ, a kind of streaked panther. April 8th praise the name of the Lord.

95 Let Eliashib rejoice with Shepherd's Purse.

Let Azbuk rejoice with Valerianella Corn Sallet.

---

[1] *Hasse*, Johann Adoph Hasse (1699–1783), a famous musician. *S.*
[2] *Col-hozeh* introduces a series of names from Neh.3 running without a break (except for one from Neh.2) to line 113.

FRAGMENT C

80 For this is a stupendous evidence of the communicating of God in externals.

For I prophecy that they will call the days by better names.

For the Lord's day is the first.

For the following is the second.

For so of the others untill the seventh.[1]

85 For the seventh day is the Sabbath according to the word of God direct for ever and ever.

For I prophecy that the King will have grace to put the crown upon the altar.

For I prophecy that the name of king in England will be given to Christ alone.

For I prophecy that men will live to a much greater age, this ripens apace God be praised.

For I prophecy that they will grow taller and stronger.

90 For degeneracy has done a great deal more than is in general imagined.

For men in David's time were ten feet high in general.

For they had degenerated also from the strength of their fathers.

For I prophecy that players and mimes will not be named amongst us.

For I prophecy in the favour of dancing which in mutual benevolence is for the glory of God.[2]

95 For I prophecy that the exactions of Moab will soon be at an end.

For the Moabites even the French are in their chastisement for humiliation.

[1] Smart returns to an idea with which he has dealt in B2.406–407.
[2] "David danced before the Lord with all his might," 2 S.6.14. *S.*

133

97 Let Geshem (which is Rain) [1] rejoice with Kneeholm. Blessed be the name of the Lord Jesus for Rain and his family and for the plenteous rain this day. April 9th 1761. N. S.

Let Bavai rejoice with Calceolus Ladies Slipper.

Let Henadad rejoice with Cacalianthemum.

100 Let Shallum rejoice with Mullein Tapsus barbatus good for the breast.

Let Ophel rejoice with Camara.

Let Meshezabeel rejoice with Stephanomelis. Old April bless the name of the Lord Jesus.

Let Zadok the son of Baana rejoice with Viburnum.

Let Vaniah rejoice with Pug in a pinner. [2] God be gracious to the house of Vane especially Anne.

105 Let Besodeiah rejoice with the Nettle.

Let Melatiah rejoice with Adonis Bird's eye.

Let Jadon rejoice with Borrage.

Let Palal rejoice with the female Balsamime. God be gracious to my wife.

Let Ezer rejoice with Basella Climbing Nightshade.

110 Let Uzai rejoice with Meadow Sweet.

Let Zalaph rejoice with Rose-bay.

Let Halohesh rejoice with Ambrosia, that bears a fruit like a club.

Let Malchiah Son of Rechab rejoice with the Rose-colour'd flowring Rush.

---

[1] There is no sanction in the Bible for any association of *Geshem* with *rain*.

[2] *Pug in a pinner* is a polyanthus; *pug* can be a term of endearment, and *pinner* a kind of woman's head-dress, so the flower-name might suggest a pretty girl in a bonnet and carry Smart's mind back once again to thoughts of Anne Hope (née Vane). *S.*

FRAGMENT C

97 For I prophecy that the Reformation will make way in France when Moab is made meek by being well drubbed by the English.

For I prophecy that the Reformation will make great way by means of the Venetians.[1]

For the Venetian will know that the Englishman is his brother.

100 For the Liturgy will obtain in all languages.

For England is the head and not the tail.

For England is the head of Europe in the spirit.

For Spain, Portugal and France are the heart.

For Holland and Germany are the middle.

105 For Italy is one of the legs.

For I prophecy that there will not be a meetinghouse within two miles of a church.

For I prophecy that schismaticks will be detected.

For I prophecy that men will learn the use of their knees.

For every thing that can be done in that posture (upon the knees) is better so done than otherwise.

110 For I prophecy that they will understand the blessing and virtue of the rain.

For rain is exceedingly good for the human body.

For it is good therefore to have flat roofs to the houses, as of old.

For it is good to let the rain come upon the naked body unto purity and refreshment.[2]

[1] Here Smart is thinking of the strained relations between the Venetian Republic and the Papacy. *S.*

[2] On worshipping in the rain, see B2.384.

JUBILATE AGNO

Let Sia rejoice with Argemone Prickly Poppy.

115 Let Lebana rejoice with Amaranthoides Globe Amaranth.

Let Rephaiah the Son of Hur rejoice with the Berry-bearing Angelica.

Let Harhaiah of the Goldsmiths rejoice with Segullum, the earth that detects the mine.

Let Harumaph rejoice with the Upright Honeysuckle.

Let Hashabniah rejoice with the Water Melon.[1] Blessed be the manuscripts of Almighty God.

120 Let Phaseah rejoice with the Cassioberry Bush.

Let Nephishesim rejoice with Cannacorus Indian Reed.

Let Tamah rejoice with Cainito Star-Apple—God be praised for this Eleventh of April O. S. in which I enter into the Fortieth Year of my age.[2] Blessed. Blessed. Blessed!

Let Siloah rejoice with Guidonia with a Rose-Colour'd-Flower.[3]

Let Benjamin a Rebuilder of Jerusalem rejoice with the Rock-Rose. Newton, bless!

125 Let Malchijah Son of Harim rejoice with Crysanthemoides.

Let Besai rejoice with Hesperis Queen's Gilly-Flow'r.

---

[1] The mottled seed of the watermelon reminds Smart once again of the ideas in B2.477–491 and C77–80.

[2] *Eleventh of April O.S.*, the date of Smart's birth in 1722; by New Style reckoning, this verse was written on 22 April 1761. *Tamah* is not a Biblical name; most probably it represents a faulty recollection of *Talmon*, from Neh.7.45. *Tamar* is another possibility, but this name does not occur in Nehemiah or Ezra, from which most of the surrounding names are drawn.

[3] This line contains a verbal coincidence with Miller's *Gardener's Dictionary*, which says that Guidonia has "a Rose-colour'd Flower." *S*.

FRAGMENT C

For I prophecy that they will respect decency in all points.

115 For they will do it in conceit,[1] word, and motion.

For they will go forth afield.

For the Devil can work upon stagnating filth to a very great degree.

For I prophecy that we shall have our horns again.[2]

For in the day of David Man as yet had a glorious horn upon his forehead.[3]

120 For this horn was a bright substance in colour & consistence as the nail of the hand.

For it was broad, thick and strong so as to serve for defence as well as ornament.

For it brightend to the Glory of God, which came upon the human face at morning prayer.

For it was largest and brightest in the best men.

For it was taken away all at once from all of them.

125 For this was done in the divine contempt of a general pusillanimity.

For this happened in a season after their return from the Babylonish captivity.[4]

---

[1] *Conceit* is used in the obsolete sense, as *thought*. S.

[2] From here to the end of Fragment C, Smart rings the changes on the idea of man's recovering his "horn." As Stead remarks, he begins with its Biblical symbolism of power, owing to its employment by animals as a weapon of attack, as in Ps.89.17: "For thou art the glory of their strength: and in thy favor our horn shall be exalted." The horn appears in many different guises and with many different meanings, some far-fetched and ridiculous. Thus there is the cornucopia in 153, while in 128 there may well be another hint of the symbolism of cuckoldry which occurred earlier in B1.46 and B1.48.

[3] *In the day of David Man as yet had a glorious horn upon his forehead*, Moses is customarily represented in Renaissance art as horned. S.

[4] The reference to *the Babylonish captivity* is important as added proof of the relationship of the *Let* and *For* verses of this fragment. The return from the Babylonian captivity is the theme of the chapters of Ezra and Nehemiah from which most of the Biblical names are drawn.

127 Let Perida rejoice with Podded Fumitory.

Let Tabbaoth rejoice with Goldy Locks. God be merciful to my wife.[1]

Let Bakbuk rejoice with Soft Thistle.

130 Let Hodevah rejoice with Coronilla.

Let Tobiah [2] rejoice with Crotolaria. God be praised for his infinite goodness & mercy.

Let Mehetabeel rejoice with Hæmanthus the Blood Flower. Blessed be the name of the Blood of the Lord Jesus.

Let Bazlith rejoice with the Horned Poppy.

Let Hagaba [3] rejoice with the Turnsole. God be gracious to Cutting.

135 Let Shalmai rejoice with Lycopersicum Love-apple. God be gracious to Dunn.

Let Arah rejoice with Fritillaria the Chequer'd Tulip.

Let Raamiah rejoice with the Double Sweetscented Pione.

Let Hashub Son of Pahath-moab rejoice with the French Honeysuckle.

Let Ananiah rejoice with the Corn-Flag.

140 Let Nahamani rejoice with the May-apple. God give me fruit to this month.

Let Mispereth rejoice with the Ring Parrakeet.

Let Nehum rejoice with the Artichoke.

Let Ginnethon [4] rejoice with the Bottle Flower.

Let Zidkijah rejoice with Mulberry Blight. God be gracious to Gum my fellow Prisoner.

---

[1] *Goldy Locks* reminds Smart of his wife, whom he had addressed in a poem as "The Lass with the Golden Locks," Callan, I, 202. S.

[2] *Tobiah*, meaning "Jah is good," may have suggested the second part of the verse.

[3] *Hagaba*, see note on C42.

[4] From this line to the end of fragment C, all the names are drawn from Neh.10.

127 For their spirits were broke and their manhood impaird by foreign vices for exaction.

For I prophecy that the English will recover their horns the first.

For I prophecy that all the nations in the world will do the like in turn.

130 For I prophecy that all Englishmen will wear their beards again.

For a beard is a good step to a horn.

For when men get their horns again, they will delight to go uncovered.

For it is not good to wear any thing upon the head.

For a man should put no obstacle between his head and the blessing of Almighty God.

135 For a hat was an abomination of the heathen. Lord have mercy upon the Quakers.[1]

For the ceiling of the house is an obstacle and therefore we pray on the house-top.

For the head will be liable to less disorders on the recovery of its horn.

For the horn on the forehead is a tower upon an arch.

For it is a strong munition against the adversary, who is sickness & death.

140 For it is instrumental in subjecting the woman.

For the insolence of the woman has increased ever since Man has been crest-fallen.

For they have turned the horn into scoff and derision without ceasing.[2]

For we are amerced of God, who has his horn.

For we are amerced of the blessed angels, who have their horns.

---

[1] Smart was thinking of the large hats worn by Quakers. S.
[2] Again the reference seems to be to the horn as symbol of cuckoldry.

145 Let Malluch rejoice with Methonica Superb Lily.

Let Jeremiah rejoice with Hemlock, which is good in outward application.

Let Bilgai rejoice with Tamalapatra Indian Leaf.

Let Maaziah rejoice with Chick Pease. God be gracious to Harris White 5th of May 1761.

Let Kelita rejoice with Xiphion the Bulbous Iris.

150 Let Pelaiah rejoice with Cloud-Berries. God be gracious to Peele and Ferry.

Let Azaniah rejoice with the Water Lily.

Let Rehob rejoice with Caucalis Bastard Parsley.

Let Sherebiah rejoice with Nigella, that bears a white flower.

Let Beninu rejoice with Heart-Pear. God be gracious to George Bening.

155 Let Bunni rejoice with Bulbine leaves like leek purple flower.

Let Zatthu rejoice with the Wild Service.

Let Hizkijah rejoice with the Dwarf American Sun-Flower.

Let Azzur rejoice with the Globe-Thistle.

Let Hariph rejoice with Summer Savoury.

160 Let Nebai rejoice with the Wild Cucumber.

Let Magpiash rejoice with the Musk.

Let Hezir rejoice with Scorpion Sena.

145 For when they get their horns again they will put them upon the altar.

For they give great occasion for mirth and musick.

For our Blessed Saviour had not his horn upon the face of the earth.

For this was in meekness & condescension to the infirmities of human nature at that time.

For at his second coming his horn will be exalted in glory.

150 For his horn is the horn of Salvation.

For Christ Jesus has exalted my voice to his own glory.

For he has answered me in the air as with a horn from Heaven to the ears of many people.

For the horn is of plenty.

For this has been the sense of all ages.

155 For Man and Earth suffer together.

For when Man was amerced of his horn, earth lost part of her fertility.

For the art of Agriculture is improving.

For this is evident in flowers.

For it is more especially manifest in double flowers.

160 For earth will get it up again by the blessing of God on the industry of man.

For the horn is of plenty because of milk & honey.

For I pray God be gracious to the Bees and the Beeves this day.

FRAGMENT D

THE surviving manuscript concludes with two double folios, numbered "10" and "11", containing on eight pages 237 lines of *Let* verses. There is no evidence either to confirm or to deny the former existence of a set of *For* verses to match. But we can be sure that composition ended on the last page of double folio 11, for the last two-thirds of the page was left blank. This portion of the poem was written between July 1762 and January 1763, at the steady rate of one line (or perhaps one pair of lines) per day.

10. Let Dew, house of Dew [1] rejoice with Xanthenes a precious stone of an amber colour.

Let Round, house of Round rejoice with Myrmeeites a gem having an Emmet in it.

Let New, house of New rejoice with Nasamonites a gem of a sanguine colour with black veins.

Let Hook, house of Hook rejoice with Sarda a Cornelian—blessed be the name of the Lord Jesus by hook.

5 Let Crook, house of Crook rejoice with Ophites black spotted marble— Blessed be the name of the Lord Jesus by crook. The Lord enable me to shift.

Let Lime, house of Lime rejoice with Sandareses a kind of gem in Pliny's list.[2]

Let Linnet, house of Linnet rejoice with Tanos, which is a mean sort of Emerald.

Let Hind, house of Hind rejoice with Pæderos Opal—God be gracious to Mrs Hind, that lived at Canbury.[3]

Let Tyrrel, house of Tyrrel rejoice with Sardius Lapis an Onyx of a black colour. God speed Hawke's Fleet.[4]

10 Let Moss, house of Moss rejoice with the Pearl-Oyster [5] behold how God has consider'd for him that lacketh.

---

[1] The choice of names in this fragment appears to be almost completely random and unsystematic, and usually they have no real association with the natural objects to which they are linked. Some are names out of Smart's past, like Richard Dongworth or Lord Vane; some were subscribers to the translation of the *Psalms*, for which the subscription-books were currently open; some were suggested merely by jingles, like Hook and Crook, Bracegirdle and Girdlestone, Graves and Tombs, or more subtly, Pelham and Holles.

[2] *Sandareses a kind of gem in Pliny's list* (generally Sandaresus); the spelling and especially the vague reference suggest that Smart is here writing from memory. S.

[3] *Canbury*, for other residents at Canonbury see C73.

[4] *God speed Hawke's fleet.* This line was probably written near the beginning of June 1762. Between April and September, Hawke was in command at Spithead and in the Bay of Biscay, but no action took place. S.

[5] *Pearl-Oyster*, probably from Anson, p. 218. S.

FRAGMENT D

Let Ross, house of Ross rejoice with the Great Flabber Dabber Flat Clapping Fish with hands. Vide Anson's Voyage & Psalm 98th ix.[1]

Let Fisher, house of Fisher rejoice with Sandastros kind of burning stone with gold drops in the body of it. God be gracious to Fisher of Cambridge & to all of his name & kindred.

Let Fuller, house of Fuller rejoice with Perileucos a precious stone with a white thread descending from its face to the bottom.

Let Thorpe, house of Thorpe rejoice with Xystios an ordinary stone of the Jasper-kind.

15 Let Alban, house of Alban rejoice with Scorpites a precious stone in some degree of the creatures.

Let Wand, house of Wand rejoice with Synochitis [2] a gem supposed by Pliny to have certain magical effects.

Let Freeman, house of Freeman rejoice with Carcinias a precious stone the colour of a sea-crab. The Lord raise the landed interest.

Let Quince, house of Quince rejoice with Onychipuncta a gem of the Jasper kind.

Let Manly, house of Manly rejoice with the Booby a tropical bird.

20 Let Fage, house of Fage rejoice with the Fiddlefish [3]—Blessed be the name of the Lord Jesus in the fish's mouth.

Let Benning, house of Benning rejoice with the Sea-Egg.[4] Lord have mercy on the soul of Benning's wife.

---

[1] *The Great Flabber Dabber Flat Clapping Fish with hands* appears to be a mixture of memory and imagination; the Flabber Dabber does not appear in Anson. Ps.98.8 (*not* 9) contains the phrase, "Let the floods clap their hands," and Smart seems to have combined this in his mind with an account of "the flat-fish, jumping a considerable height out of the water," Anson, p. 217. *S.* Also in Anson (following p. 122) is a curious engraving of sea-lions in which their appearance might be appropriate to the Flabber Dabber; while the description on p. 123 says that the flippers of these animals "are divided at the ends like fingers . . . and each of these extremities is furnished with a nail."

[2] *Synochitis* recurs in D71, as "a stone abused by ancient sorcerers"; when ghosts were raised, the stone could be used to keep them above ground, as Pliny reports with some scepticism. *S.*

[3] *Fiddlefish*, Anson, p. 265.

[4] *Sea-Egg*, Anson, p. 265. Benning's wife may be the wife of the George Bening mentioned in C154. *S.*

JUBILATE AGNO

Let Singleton, house of Singleton rejoice with the Hog-Plump.[1] Lord have mercy on the soul of Lord Vane.

Let Thickness, house of Thickness rejoice with The Papah a fruit found at Chequetan.[2]

Let Heartly, house of Heartly rejoice with the Drummer-Fish. God be gracious to Heartly of Christ, to Marsh, Hingeston & Bill.[3]

25 Let Sizer, house of Sizer rejoice with Trichros a precious stone black at bottom, white atop and blood-red in the middle.

Let Chetwind, house of Chetwind rejoice with Hammocrysos, a gem with gold sands on it.

Let Branch, house of Branch rejoice with Hæmatites—Blessed be the name of the Lord Jesus THE BRANCH.[4]

Let Dongworth, house of Dongworth rejoice with Rhymay the Bread-fruit.[5] God be gracious to the immortal soul of Richard Dongworth.

Let Randall, house of Randall rejoice with Guavoes. God give Randall success.[6]

30 Let Osborne, house of Osborne rejoice with Lithizontes a sort of carbuncle. God be gracious to the Duke of Leeds [7] & his family.

Let Oldcastle, house of Oldcastle rejoice with Leucopthalmos. God put it in heart of king to repair & beautify Dover Castle.

---

[1] *Hog-Plump*, "a small plumb of an agreeable acid," Anson, p. 267. *Lord Vane* was the proprietor of the estates of which Smart's father was steward. *S.* There is no apparent link between Lord Vane and the house of Singleton.

[2] *Papah a fruit found at Chequetan*, Anson, p. 267. *S.*

[3] *Marsh, Hingeston & Bill* all subscribed to the *Psalms. S.*

[4] *The Lord Jesus THE BRANCH*: twice in the Bible the word Branch is completely capitalized, in Zec.3.8 and 6.12. In the Targum on Zec., the term is interpreted as "the Messiah." Smart capitalizes Branch again in precisely this sense in his translation of Ps.132 (Callan, II, 745).

[5] *Rhymay the Bread-fruit*, Anson, p. 310, and the following plate; Anson spells it *Rima. Richard Dongworth* was Master of Durham School when Smart studied there, and had died in February 1761, a little more than a year before this entry. *S.* It may not be too fantastic to suppose that *Rhymay* suggested the name of Dongworth's immediate predecessor at Durham, John Rymer; see also the note on the next line.

[6] *Guavoes*, Anson, p. 310. *Randall* may be John Randall, professor of music at Cambridge, who composed music for some of Smart's *Psalms. S.* He may also be Thomas Randall, who became Master of Durham School on Dongworth's death.

[7] *Osborne*, the family name of the Dukes of Leeds.

146

FRAGMENT D

Let Beeson, house of Beeson rejoice with Pyropus, carbuncle opal. God be gracious to Masters of Yoke's Place.

Let Salmon, house of Salmon rejoice with Sapinos a kind of Amethyst.

Let Crutenden, house of Crutenden rejoice with Veneris Gemma a kind of amethyst.

35 Let Bridges, house of Bridges rejoice with Jasponyx, which is the Jasper-Onyx.

Let Lane, house of Lane rejoice with Myrmecias a precious stone with little knots in it.

Let Cope, house of Cope rejoice with Centipedes God give me strength to cope with all my adversaries.

Let Sutton, house of Sutton rejoice with Cholos a gem of the Emerald kind.

Let Pelham, house of Pelham rejoice with Callimus in Taphiusio one stone in the body of another. God bless the Duke of Newcastle.[1]

40 Let Holles, house of Holles rejoice with Pyriasis a black stone that burns by friction. The Lord kindle amongst Englishmen a sense of their name.

Let Lister, house of Lister rejoice with Craterites a very hard stone. The Lord hear my prayer even as I attend unto his commandments.

Let Ash, house of Ash rejoice with Callaica, a green gem. God be gracious to Miss Leroche my fellow traveler from Calais.[2]

Let Baily, house of Baily rejoice with Catopyrites of Cappadocia. God be gracious to the immortal soul of Lewes Baily [3] author of the Practice of Piety.

---

[1] *Pelham, Holles:* Thomas Pelham, Baron Pelham of Laughton, took the name of Holles in addition to Pelham on inheriting the Holles estate in 1711, and in 1715 he was created Duke of Newcastle. This would be well known to Smart, as the Duke was chancellor of Cambridge from 1748 to 1768, and moreover the houses of Newcastle and Vane were closely related.

[2] *My fellow traveler from Calais*, the only known record of any Continental trip by Smart. *S.*

[3] *Lewes Baily* was Lewis Bayly, Bishop of Bangor, whose devotional work, *The Practice of Piety*, was first published about 1613 (no copy of the first edition is known to survive). It went through innumerable editions in the seventeenth and eighteenth centuries. *S.*

JUBILATE AGNO

Let Glover, house of Glover rejoice with Capnites a kind of Jasper blessed be the memory of Glover the martyr.[1]

45 Let Egerton, house of Egerton rejoice with Sphragis green but not pellucid.

Let Reading, house of Reading rejoice with Synodontites found in the fish Synodontes. 27th July N. S. 1762. Lord Jesus have mercy on my soul.

Let Bolton, house of Bolton rejoice with Polygrammos, a kind of Jasper with white streaks.

Let Paulet, house of Paulet rejoice with Chalcites, a precious stone of the colour of Brass.

Let Stapleton, house of Stapleton rejoice with Scythis a precious stone the Lord rebuild the old houses of England.

50 Let Newdigate, house of Newdigate rejoice with Sandaserion a stone in India like Green Oil.

Let Knightly, house of Knightly rejoice with Zoronysios a gem supposed by the ancients to have magical effects. Star—word—herb—gem.

Let Fellows, house of Fellows rejoice with Syrites a gem found in a Wolf's bladder.

Let Ascham, house of Ascham rejoice with Thyitis a precious stone remarkably hard. God be gracious to Bennet.[2]

Let Mowbray, house of Mowbray rejoice with The Black & Blue Creeper a beautiful small bird of Brazil.

55 Let Aldrich, house of Aldrich rejoice with the Trincalo or Tricolor, a leaf without a flower or the flower of a leaf.

Let Culmer, house of Culmer rejoice with Phloginos a gem of a fire-colour.

Let Catesby, house of Catesby rejoice with Cerites a precious stone like wax.

---

[1] Robert Glover was burnt at Coventry in 1555, and is one of the martyrs mentioned in Bayly's *Practice of Piety. S.*

[2] James Bennet's edition of *The English Works of Roger Ascham* (for which Johnson wrote the Life and the dedication) was published by John Newbery in association with Davies and the Dodsleys in 1761.

FRAGMENT D

Let Atterbury, house of Atterbury rejoice with Eurotias a black stone with the appearance of mould on it.

Let Hoare, house of Hoare rejoice with Crysopis a precious stone of a gold-colour. God be gracious to John Rust.

60 Let Fane, house of Fane rejoice with Chalcedonius Lapis a sort of onyx called Chalcedony.

Let Lorman, house of Lorman rejoice with Cheramites, a sort of precious stone.

Let Flexney, house of Flexney rejoice with Triopthalmos—God be gracious to Churchill, Loyd and especially to Sheels.[1]

Let Gavel, house of Gavel rejoice with Phlogites a precious stone of a various flame-colour.

Let Hederick, house of Hederick rejoice with Pyritis a precious stone which held in the hand will burn it; this is fixed fire.

65 Let Pleasant, house of Pleasant rejoice with The Carrier Fish—God be gracious to Dame Fysh.[2]

Let Tayler, house of Tayler rejoice with the Flying Mole—God keep him from the poor man's garden. God be gracious to William Tayler Sen & Junr.

Let Grieve, house of Grieve rejoice with Orites a precious stone perfectly round. Blessed be the name of the Man of Melancholy,[3] for Jacob Grieve.

Let Bowes, house of Bowes rejoice with the Dog Fly.[4] Lord have mercy upon me & support me in all my plagues & temptations.

---

[1] *Flexney* is William Flexney (d. 1808), one of the booksellers named in the imprint of Smart's *Psalms* (1765). Flexney also published many of the poems of Charles Churchill; at least one poem by Robert Lloyd, *An Epistle to C. Churchill* (1761); and the only work of the Rev. James Sheeles to be separately published, his *Sermon . . . on Friday, March 12, 1762* (1762). Smart later composed an epitaph on Sheeles (Callan, I, 36), who died 29 October 1762. Evidently Smart was fully aware of the publishing arrangements made by all three authors with Flexney.

[2] *Dame Fysh*, see also B1.114.

[3] *The Man of Melancholy* may equal the Man of Sorrows. *S.*

[4] *Dog Fly*, the English translation of a Greek word which meant either a dog-fly or a "shameless fly," an abusive epithet for an impudent woman. The secondary meaning may have prompted the reference to his "plagues & temptations." *S.*

JUBILATE AGNO

Let Alberton, house of Alberton rejoice with Paneros a precious stone good against barrenness.

70 Let Morgan, house of Morgan rejoice with Prasius Lapis of a Leek-green colour.[1]

Let Powell, house of Powell rejoice with Synochitis [2] a precious stone abused by the ancient sorcerers.

Let Howell, house of Howell rejoice with Ostracias a gem like an oyster.

Let Close, house of Close rejoice with Chalcophonos a gem sounding like brass. O all ye gems of the mine bless ye the Lord, praise him & magnify him for ever.[3]

Let Johnson, house of Johnson rejoice with Omphalocarpa a kind of bur God be gracious to Samuel Johnson.[4]

75 Let Hopgood, house of Hopgood rejoice with Nepenthes an herb which infused in wine drives away sadness—very likely.[5]

Let Hopwood, house of Hopwood rejoice with Aspalathus the Rose o Jerusalem.

Let Benson, house of Benson rejoice with Sea-Ragwort or Powder'd Bean. Lord have mercy on the soul of Dr Benson Bsp. of Gloucester.[6]

Let Marvel, house of Marvel rejoice with Brya a little shrub like birch.

Let Hull, house of Hull rejoice with Subis a bird called the Spight which breaks the Eagle's eggs.

80 Let Mason, house of Mason rejoice with Suberies the Capitol Cork Tree Lord be merciful to William Mason.[7]

---

[1] A Welsh name is properly associated with a *leek-green* stone.

[2] *Synochitis*, see D16.

[3] The latter part of the line is an adaptation of the Benedicite in the Book of Common Prayer, "O all ye Works of the Lord, bless ye the Lord: praise Him, and magnify Him forever." S.

[4] *Samuel Johnson* had not yet become the Doctor; the date of his visit to Smart is the asylum is not known, but it may well have occurred near this time (August-September 1762), prompting this entry. S.

[5] *Very likely* is added in Smart's hand in a different ink, perhaps as a mark of scepticism on second thoughts.

[6] *Martin Benson*, Bishop of Gloucester, had been Canon of Durham during Smart's school-days. S.

[7] *William Mason* was Thomas Gray's friend and correspondent, and had been addressed by Smart in the fable, "The Brocaded Gown and Linen Rag" (Callan, I 49–50). S.

FRAGMENT D

Let Fountain, house of Fountain rejoice with Syriacus Rephanus a sweet kind of Radish.

Let Scroop, house of Scroop rejoice with Fig-Wine—Palmi primarium vinum. Not so—Palmi-primum is the word.[1]

Let Hollingstead, house of Hollingstead rejoice with Sissitietæris herb of good fellowship. Praise the name of the Lord September 1762.

Let Moyle, house of Moyle rejoice with Phlox a flame-colour'd flower without smell. tentanda via est.[2] Via, veritas, vita sunt Christus.

85 Let Mount, house of Mount rejoice with Anthera a flowering herb. The Lord lift me up.

Let Dowers, house of Dowers rejoice with The American Nonpareil a beautiful small bird.

Let Cudworth, house of Cudworth rejoice with the Indian Jaca Tree, which bears large clusters of fruit like apples.

Let Cuthbert, house of Cuthbert rejoice with Phyllandrian a good herb growing in marshes—Lord have mercy on the soul of Cornelius Harrison.

Let Chillingworth, house of Chillingworth rejoice with Polygonoides an herb with leaves like laurel long & thick good against serpents.

90 Let Conworth, house of Conworth rejoice with Nenuphar a kind of Water Lily.

Let Ransom, house of Ransom rejoice with Isiclos Plocamos a sea shrub of the Coral kind, or rather like Coral.

Let Ponder, house of Ponder rejoice with Polion an herb, whose leaves are white in the morning, purple at noon, & blue in the evening.

Let Woodward, house of Woodward rejoice with Nerium the Rose-Laurel—God make the professorship of fossils in Cambridge a useful thing.[3]

Let Spincks, house of Spincks rejoice with Strathiomela a little sort of Quinces—The Lord Jesus pray for me.

---

[1] *Not so . . . word* is evidently a later addition in the ink of *Very likely*, D75. Stead takes this as an indication that Smart was writing from memory.

[2] *Tentanda via est* is an echo of Virgil, *Georgics*, III.8.

[3] *Woodward . . . professorship of fossils in Cambridge*, see B1.279–280 and note.

95 Let Peacock, house of Peacock rejoice with Engalacton an herb good to breed milk.

Let Nason, house of Nason rejoice with Errhinum a medicine to clear the nose.

Let Bold, house of Bold rejoice with the Hop-Hornbeam. God send me a neighbour this September.

Let Spriggings, house of Spriggings rejoice with Eon the Tree of which Argo was built.

Let Bear, house of Bear rejoice with Gelotophyllis an herb which drank in wine & myrrh causes excess of laughter.

100 Let Sloper, house of Sloper rejoice with Gelotophye another laughing plant.

Let Tollfree, house of Tollfree rejoice with Fern of Trees—Lord stave off evil this day.

Let Clare, house of Clare rejoice with Galeotes a kind of Lizard at enmity with serpents. Lord receive the soul of Dr Wilcox Master of Clare Hall.[1]

Let Wilmot, house of Wilmot rejoice with Epipetros an herb coming up spontaneous (of the seed of the earth) but never flowers.

Let Anstey, house of Anstey rejoice with Eumeces a kind of balm. Lord have mercy on Christopher Anstey & his kinswoman.

105 Let Ruston, house of Ruston rejoice with Fulviana Herba, ab inventore good to provoke urine. Lord have mercy upon Roger Pratt & his family.[2]

Let Atwood, house of Atwood rejoice with Rhodora with leaves like a nettle and flower like a rose. God bless all benefactors of Pembroke Hall.[3]

Let Shield, house of Shield rejoice with Reseda herb dissolving swelling, and imposthumes.

Let Atkins, house of Atkins rejoice with Salicastrum Wild Wine upon willows & osiers.

---

[1] *John Wilcox, Master of Clare Hall*, died 16 September 1762 (*S.*) and this line was most probably written on 20 September.

[2] *Roger Pratt* Esq. of Ruston Hall subscribed to the *Psalms. S.* His estate may be the Ruston referred to in B1.33.

[3] *Richard Atwood* (d. 1734) was a notable benefactor of Pembroke College (Venn, *Alumni Cantabrigiensis*, I, 55).

FRAGMENT D

Let Pearson, house of Pearson rejoice with the American Aloe. I pray for the soul of Frances Burton.

110 Let Hough, house of Hough rejoice with Pegasus The Flying Horse there be millions of them in the air.[1] God bless the memories of Bsp. Hough & of Peter.

Let Evelyn, house of Evelyn [2] rejoice with Phu a Plinian shrub sweet-scented. I pray God for trees enough in the posterities.

Let Wing, house of Wing rejoice with Phlomos a sort of Rush. I give the glory to God, thro Christ, for taking the Havannah.[3] Septr 30th 1762.

Let Chace, house of Chace rejoice with Papyrus. God be gracious to Sr Richard & family.

Let Pulteney, house of Pulteney rejoice with Tragion a shrub like Juniper.

115 Let Abdy, house of Abdy rejoice with Ecbolia a medicine to fetch a dead child out of the womb. God give me to bless for Gulstone & Halford.

Let Hoadley, house of Hoadley rejoice with Dryas Hyphear which is the Oak-Missletoe.

Let Free, house of Free rejoice with Thya a kind of Wild Cypress.

Let Pink, house of Pink rejoice with Trigonum herb used in garlands—the Lord succeed my pink borders.[4]

Let Somner, house of Somner rejoice with the Blue Daisie [5]—God be gracious to my neighbour & his family this day, 7th Octr 1762.

120 Let Race, house of Race rejoice with Osiritis Dogshead. God be praised for the eighth of October 1762.

Let Trowell, house of Trowell rejoice with Teachites kind of sweet rush.

Let Tilson, house of Tilson rejoice with Teramnos a kind of weed. Lord have mercy on the soul of Tilson Fellow of Pembroke Hall.

---

[1] *Pegasus The Flying Horse. There be millions of them in the air;* probably written on 28 September, the Eve of St. Michael and All Angels; that is, the air is full of angels. *S.*

[2] *Evelyn* naturally suggests John Evelyn's *Sylva*, leading to the reference to trees. *S.*

[3] *Havannah:* Admiral Sir George Pocock appeared before Havana on 6 June 1762 and forced its surrender on 13 August. The news was announced in the *London Gazette*, 30 September. Smart addressed an ode to Pocock on the occasion (Callan, I, 13-15). *S.*

[4] *The Lord succeed my pink borders,* see B2.492, note.

[5] *The Blue Daisie* must be the Michaelmas Daisy, especially in view of the date. *S.*

Let Loom, house of Loom rejoice with Calocasia, an Egyptian Bean of whose leaves they made cups & pots.

Let Knock, house of Knock rejoice with Condurdon [1] which bears red flowers in July & worn about the neck is good for scrophulous cases.

125 Let Case, house of Case rejoice with Coctanum a Syrian Fig. The Lord care for my cough.

Let Tomlyn, house of Tomlyn rejoice with Tetralix a kind of herb.

Let Bason, house of Bason rejoice with Thelypteris which is Sea-Fern.

Let Joslyn, house of Joslyn rejoice with Cotonea a Venetian herb.

11. Let Mace, house of Mace rejoice with Adipsos a kind of Green Palm with the smell of a quince.

130 Let Potts, house of Potts rejoice with Ulex an herb like rosemary with a quality of attracting gold.

Let Bedingfield, house of Bedingfield rejoice with Zygia, which is a kind of maple.

Let Tough, house of Tough rejoice with Accipitrina. N. B. The Hawk beat the raven S[t] Luke's day 1762. [2]

Let Balsam, house of Balsam rejoice with Chenomycon an herb the sight of which terrifies a goose. Lord have mercy on William Hunter his family.

Let Graves, house of Graves rejoice with Cinnaris the Stag's antidote the persecuted Christian is as the hunted stag.

135 Let Tombs, house of Tombs rejoice with Acesis Water Sage—God be gracious to Christopher Charles Tombs.

Let Addy, house of Addy rejoice with Crysippea a kind of herb so called from the discoverer.

Let Jump, house of Jump rejoice with Zoster a Sea-Shrub. Blessed be the name of Christ for the Anniversary of the Battle of Agincourt [3] 1762.

Let Bracegirdle, house of Bracegirdle rejoice with Xiris a kind of herb with sharp leaves.

---

[1] *Condurdon* occurs again in D227.

[2] *Accipitrina*, hawkweed. *S. The hawk beat the raven* is unexplained. *St. Luke's day*, 18 October.

[3] *Battle of Agincourt*, 25 October.

FRAGMENT D

Let Girdlestone, house of Girdlestone rejoice with Crysocarpum a kind of Ivy.

140 Let Homer, house of Homer rejoice with Cinnabar which makes a red colour.

Let Lenox, house of Lenox rejoice with Achnas the Wild Pear Tree. God be gracious to the Duke of Richmond.[1]

Let Altham, house of Altham rejoice with the Everlasting Apple-Tree.

Let Travell, house of Travell rejoice with Ciborium The Egyptian Bean.

Let Tyers, house of Tyers rejoice with Ægilops a kind of bulbous root. God give good will to Jonathan Tyers & his family this day. All Saints.[2] N. S. 1762.

145 Let Clever, house of Clever rejoice with Calathiana a sort of Autumnal flower.

Let Bones, house of Bones rejoice with The Red-Crested Black & Blue Bird of Surinam.

Let Pownall, house of Pownall rejoice with the Murrion [3] a creature of the Beaver kind.

Let Fig, house of Fig rejoice with Fleawort. The Lord magnify the idea of Smart singing hymns on this day in the eyes of the whole University of Cambridge. Novr 5th 1762. N. S.[4]

Let Codrington, house of Codrington rejoice with Thelyphonon an herb whose root kills scorpions.

150 Let Butler, house of Butler rejoice with Theombrotios a Persian herb. God be gracious to the immortal Soul of the Duke of Ormond.[5]

Let Bodley, house of Bodley rejoice with Tetragnathius a creature of the Spider kind.

Let Acton, house of Acton rejoice with Theangelis an herb used by the Ancients for magical purposes.

---

[1] *Lenox* (Lennox), the family name of the Dukes of Richmond.
[2] *All Saints*, 1 November. *Jonathan Tyers* was also cited in B2.455. *S.*
[3] *Murrion*, a variant of morion, a helmet without a beaver. *S.*
[4] This line is the only place in which Smart's own name occurs in the whole MS., and it is characteristic that he should picture himself singing hymns before his University. Probably he was thinking of and had begun work on his metrical Psalms and their accompanying Hymns. *S.*
[5] *Butler*, the family name of the Dukes of Ormond; the last Duke died in 1758.

Let Peckwater, house of Peckwater rejoice with Tettigonia a small kind of Grashopper.

Let Sheldon, house of Sheldon rejoice with Teucrion an herb like Germander.

155 Let Brecknock, house of Brecknock rejoice with Thalassegle an herb. God be merciful to Timothy Brecknock.

Let Plank, house of Plank rejoice with the Sea Purslaine—God be gracious to Thomas Rosoman & family.

Let Goosetree, house of Goosetree rejoice with Hippophaes a kind of teazle used in the dressing of cloth. God exalt the Soul of Captain Goosetree.

Let Baimbridge, house of Baimbridge rejoice with Hippophæstum of the same kind. Horses shou'd be clock'd in winter.[1]—Bambridge praise the name of the Lord.

Let Metcalf, house of Metcalf rejoice with Holcus Wall-Barley—God give grace to my adversaries to ask council of Abel.[2]

160 Let Graner, house of Graner rejoice with Hircules Bastard Nard. The Lord English Granier & his family.[3]

Let Cape, house of Cape rejoice with Orgament an herb.

Let Oram, house of Oram rejoice with Helus an herb like unto Orgament.

Let Sykes, house of Sykes rejoice with Hadrobolum a kind of sweet gum.

Let Plumer, house of Plumer rejoice with Hastula Regia an herb resembling a spear.

165 Let Digby, house of Digby rejoice with Glycyrhiza a Sweetroot. God be gracious to Sᵣ Digby Legard his Son & family.

---

[1] *Horses shou'd be clock'd in winter* evidently means that they should be cloaked or blanketed. *Clocking a horse* in the sense of timing his speed is a late nineteenth-century usage.

[2] *Smart's adversaries* are apparently those who had him committed to the asylum; after his release he wanted to bring suit against them. *S. God give grace to my adversaries to ask council of Abel*, that is, give them grace to make an end (of Smart's confinement); the reference is to 2 S.20.18. This appears to be an indication that by mid-November of 1762 some move was afoot to secure Smart's release, an event which took place early in the new year.

[3] *The Lord English Granier* probably means to make English, to naturalize. *S.* But it may be that Smart mistakenly omitted the word *bless* before *English*.

FRAGMENT D

Let Otway, house of Otway rejoice with Hippice an herb which being held in an horse's mouth keeps him from hunger.

Let Cecil, house of Cecil rejoice with Gnaphalium an herb bleached by nature white & soft for the purpose of flax. God bless Lord Salisbury.[1]

Let Rogers, house of Rogers rejoice with Hypelates a kind of Laurel— God be gracious to Rogers & Spilsbury with their families.

Let Cambden, house of Cambden rejoice with Glischromargos a kind of white marl.

170 Let Conduit, house of Conduit rejoice with Græcula a kind of Rose. God be gracious to the immortal Soul of Sr Isaac Newton.

Let Hands, house of Hands rejoice with Hadrosphærum a kind of Spikenard with broad leaves.

Let Snipe, house of Snipe rejoice with Hæmotimon a kind of red glass. Blessed be the name of Jesus for the 29th of Nov^r.

Let Aylesworth, house of Aylesworth rejoice with Glinon which is a kind of Maple.

Let Aisley, house of Aisley rejoice with Halicastrum which is a kind of bread corn.

175 Let Ready, house of Ready rejoice with Junco The Reed Sparrow. blessed be the name of Christ Jesus Voice & Instrument.

Let Bland, house of Bland rejoice with Lacta a kind of Cassia. God be gracious to Bland of Durham & the Widow George.

Let Abington, house of Abington rejoice with Lea a kind of Colewort praise him upon the sound of the trumpet.

Let Adcock, house of Adcock rejoice with Lada a shrub, which has gummy leaves.

Let Snow, house of Snow rejoice with Hysginum [2] a plant dying Scarlet.

180 Let Wardell, house of Wardell rejoice with Leiostreum a smooth oyster. God give grace to the black trumpeter & have mercy on the soul of Scipio.[3]

---

[1] *Cecil*, the family name of the Earls of Salisbury.
[2] *Hysgimum* is not a plant but a dye, and not scarlet but crimson. *S.*
[3] *The black trumpeter:* as a surmise, the trumpet in D177 brought to Smart's mind a negro trumpeter whose name was Scipio; but no such person has been identified. *S.*

Let Herring, house of Herring rejoice with Iberica a kind of herb. blessed be the name of the Lord Jesus for Miss Herring.

Let Dolben, house of Dolben rejoice with Irio Winter Cresses, Rock Gentle or Rock Gallant.

Let Oakley, house of Oakley [1] rejoice with the Skink a little amphibious creature found upon Nile.

Let Owen, house of Owen rejoice with the Shag-green [2] a beast from which the skin so called is taken.

185 Let Twist, house of Twist rejoice with Neottophora a little creature that carries its young upon its back.

Let Constant, house of Constant rejoice with the Musk-Goat—I bless God for two visions of Anne Hope's being in charity with me. [3]

Let Amos, house of Amos rejoice with The Avosetta [4] a bird found at Rome.

Let Humphreys, house of Humphreys rejoice with The Beardmanica a curious bird.

Let Busby, house of Busby [5] rejoice with The Ganser a bird. God prosper Westminster-School.

190 Let Alured, house of Alured rejoice with the Book-Spider—I refer the people of both Universitys to the Bible for their morality.

Let Lidgate, house of Lidgate rejoice with The Flammant a curious large bird on the coast of Cuba. God make us amends for the restoration of the Havannah. [6]

---

[1] *Oakley* recurs in D211.

[2] *Shag-green*, shagreen, a kind of leather but not a beast. *S*.

[3] It is worth noting that *Constant* in this passage leads on to Anne Hope. *S*. See B2.534.

[4] The *Avosetta* and the next eleven birds cited by Smart (excepting the mistake in D193) are found in Albin. *S*. Surely this concentration is too great for mere coincidence.

[5] *Busby*, Richard Busby (1606–1695) was probably the most celebrated master of Westminster School.

[6] *Havannah:* Smart had noted the capture of Havana in D112. It was restored to Spain by the Treaty of Paris, 10 February 1763, announced in *Gentleman's Magazine* in March. But as Smart was writing this section pretty regularly at one line per day, this line must have been written about 18 December 1762, so he must be referring merely to the fact that a restoration had been proposed. This has some confirmation in the next line, where he prays for the prospective treaty of peace. *S*.

FRAGMENT D

Let Cunningham, house of Cunningham rejoice with The Bohemian Jay.
I pray for peace between the K. of Prussia & Empress Queen.

Let Thornhill, house of Thornhill rejoice with The Albicore a Sea Bird.[1]
God be gracious to Hogarth his wife. Blessed be the name of the Lord
Jesus at Adgecomb.

Let Dawn, house of Dawn rejoice with The Frigate Bird which is found
upon the coasts of India.

195 Let Horton, house of Horton rejoice with Birdlime [2]—Blessed be the
name of the Lord Jesus against the destruction of Small Birds.

Let Arne, house of Arne[3] rejoice with The Jay of Bengal. God be gracious
to Arne his wife to Michael & Charles Burney.

Let Westbrooke, house of Westbrooke rejoice with the Quail of Bengal.
God be gracious to the people of Maidstone.[4]

Let Allcock, house of Allcock rejoice with The King of the Wavows a
strange fowl. I pray for the whole University of Cambridge especially
Jesus College this blessed day.[5]

Let Audley, house of Audley rejoice with The Green Crown Bird. The
Lord help on with the hymns.[6]

200 Let Bloom, house of Bloom rejoice with Hecatompus a fish with an
hundred feet.

Let Beacon, house of Beacon rejoice with Amadavad a fine bird in the East
Indies.

---

[1] The *Albicore* is a fish, not a bird. *S. Hogarth his wife:* in 1729 William Hogarth
made a runaway marriage with Jane, only daughter of Sir James Thornhill; it was a
marriage as famous as Garrick's for its felicity.

[2] *Birdlime* is the adhesive spread on twigs to ensnare small birds, leading Smart to
an invocation against this cruel practice. *S.*

[3] *Arne* was the musician Thomas Augustine Arne, one of whose pupils was Dr.
Charles Burney, who was also Smart's faithful friend. *S.*

[4] *Maidstone* was the scene of Smart's earliest schooling, before he went to Durham.
S.

[5] *The King of the Wavows* is the Indian vulture, at least one specimen of which had
been exhibited in London (Albin, II, 4). *S. Jesus College* was founded in 1496 by
John Alcock, Bishop of Ely.

[6] *The hymns* are the "Hymns and Spiritual Songs" which formed part of the volume
of *Psalms* (1765).

159

JUBILATE AGNO

Let Blomer, house of Blomer rejoice with Halimus a Shrub to hedge with. Lord have mercy upon poor labourers this bitter frost [1] Dec.ʳ 29 N. S. 1762.

Let Merrick, house of Merrick [2] rejoice with Lageus a kind of Grape. God all-sufficient bless & forward the Psalmist in the Lord Jesus.

Let Appleby, house of Appleby rejoice with Laburnum a shrub whose blossom is disliked by bees.

205 Let Waite, house of Waite rejoice with the Shittah-Tree—blessed be the name of the Lord Jesus for the musicians & dancers this holiday-time. [3]

Let Stedman, house of Stedman rejoice with Jacobæa S.ᵗ James's Wort. God be merciful to the house of Stuart. [4]

Let Poet, house of Poet rejoice with Hedrychum a kind of ointment of a sweet smelling savour. God speed the New Year thro' Christ 1763.

Let Jesse, house of Jesse rejoice with the Lawrey a kind of bird. God forward my version of the psalms thro' Jesus Christ our Lord.

Let Clemison, house of Clemison rejoice with Helia a kind of Ivy. God be praised for the vision of the Redcap & packet. [5]

210 Let Crockatt, house of Crockatt rejoice with Emboline an Asiatic Shrub with small leaves an antidote. I pray for the soul of Crockatt the bookseller [6] the first to put me upon a version of the Psalms.

Let Oakley, house of Oakley [7] rejoice with Haliphæus a tree with such bitter fruit that nothing but swine will touch it.

Let Preacher, house of Preacher rejoice with Helvella a small sort of cabbage. God be merciful to the immortal soul of Stephen Preacher.

---

[1] *This bitter frost* was the great frost of December 1762, described in *Gentleman's Magazine* (1763), p. 42. *S.*

[2] *Merrick* is James Merrick (1720–1769), whose verse-translation of the Psalms antedated Smart's and was more highly praised by contemporary critics (see Brittain, p. 277). Even while preoccupied with his own version (see D208), Smart had a good word for his rival.

[3] *Waite* reminds Smart of the waits or carollers of the Christmas season—or did the process run in the opposite direction?

[4] *House of Stuart*, see also B1.71.

[5] *The vision of the Redcap & packet* is unexplained.

[6] *Crockatt the bookseller* was James Crokat or Crokatt, whose publishing activities ended some ten years before this entry, so that Smart's metrical Psalms was a project of long standing. *S.*

[7] *Oakley* appears also in D183.

160

FRAGMENT D

Let Heron, house of Heron rejoice with the Junal-Tree on which the Cochineal feeds.

Let Kitcat, house of Kitcat rejoice with Copec the Pitch-Stone. Janry 8th 1763 Hallelujah.

215 Let Gisbourne, house of Gisbourne rejoice with Isocinnamon an herb of a sweet smelling savour.

Let Poor, house of Poor rejoice with Jasione a kind of Withwind—Lord have mercy on the poor this hard weather.[1] Jan: 10th 1763.

Let Eccles, house of Eccles rejoice with Heptapleuros a kind of Plantaine. I pray for a musician or musicians to set the new psalms.

Let Moseley, house of Moseley rejoice with Spruce—I bless God for Old Foundation Day [2] at Pemb. Hall.

Let Pass, house of Pass rejoice with Salt—The Lord pass the last year's accounts in my conscience thro' the merits of Jesus Christ. New Year by Old Stile [3] 1763.

220 Let Forward, house of Forward rejoice with Immussulus a kind of bird the Lord forward my translation of the psalms this year.

Let Quarme, house of Quarme rejoice with Thyosiris yellow Succory— I pray God bless all my Subscribers.

Let Larkin, house of Larkin rejoice with Long-wort or Torch-herb—God give me good riddance of my present grievances.

Let Halford, house of Halford rejoice with Siren a musical bird. God consider thou me for the baseness of those I have served very highly.

Let Ayerst, house of Ayerst rejoice with the Wild Beet—God be gracious to Smith, Cousins, Austin, Cam & Kingsley & Kinleside.

225 Let Decker, house of Decker rejoice with Sirpe a Cyrenian plant yielding an odoriferous juice.

Let Cust, house of Cust rejoice with Margaris a date like unto a pearl.

---

[1] *This hard weather:* the cold of late December continued into January, and on the 11th a man was found frozen to death in Fleet Ditch; *Gentleman's Magazine* (1763), p. 43.
[2] *Old Foundation Day*, a college festival at the New Year. S.
[3] *New Year by Old Stile* is 12 January. S.

JUBILATE AGNO

Let Usher, house of Usher rejoice with Condurdon [1] an herb with a red flower worn about the neck for the scurvy.

Let Slingsby, house of Slingsby rejoice with Midas a little worm breeding in beans.

Let Farmer, house of Farmer rejoice with Merois an herb growing at Meroe leaf like lettuce & good for dropsy.

230 Let Affleck, house of Affleck [2] rejoice with The Box-thorn. Blessed be the name of the Lord Jesus Emanuel.

Let Arnold, house of Arnold rejoice with Leucographis a simple good against spitting of blood.

Let Morris, house of Morris rejoice with Lepidium a Simple of the Cress kind.

Let Crane, house of Crane rejoice with Libanotis an herb that smells like Frankinsense.

Let Arden, house of Arden rejoice with Mew an herb with the stalk & leaves like Anise.

235 Let Joram, house of Joram rejoice with Meliphylla Balm Gentle   God be gracious to John Sherrat. [3]

---

[1] *Condurdon* appears also in D124.

[2] *Affleck*, William Affleck (d. 1806) became Fellow of Emmanuel Hall in 1739, the year of Smart's matriculation at Pembroke.

[3] *John Sherrat:* As Stead points out, this citation of John Sherratt is most significant, occurring just before the close of *Jubilate Agno*, and probably written near the end of January 1763. Efforts to gain Smart's release apparently began in the preceding year (for example, see D159), and Smart himself later testified that Sherratt played a leading role in their successful outcome. "An Epistle to John Sherratt, Esq." (Callan, I, 211–213), is most specific:

> "Well nigh seven years had fill'd their tale,
> From Winter's urn to Autumn's scale,
> And found no friend to grief and *Smart*,
> Like Thee and Her, thy sweeter part:
>
> *   *   *
>
> 'Tis well to signalize a deed,
> And have no precedent to plead;
> 'Tis blessing as by God we're told,
> To come and visit friends in hold;
> Which skill is greater in degree,
> If goodness set the prisoner free.
> 'Tis you that have in my behalf,
> Produc'd the robe and kill'd the calf;
> Have hail'd the *restoration day*,
> And bid the loudest music play."

FRAGMENT D

Let Odwell, house of Odwell rejoice with Lappago Maiden Lips. Blessed be the name of Jesus in singularities & singular mercies.

Let Odney, house of Odney rejoice with Canaria a simple called Hound's-grass.[1]

[1] Here the MS. breaks off only part of the way down the page, so that it is obviously the end and not simply a defect of text. At one line per day, the apparent rate of composition of this part of the poem, the last line was written on 30 January 1763, which we may reasonably assume to be very nearly the date of Smart's release from the asylum.

TEXTUAL NOTES

THIS table lists all points at which the present edition differs verbally from that edited by William Force Stead. It also records all the author's deletions, indicates all words and letters which he inserted, and lists all slips of the pen which have been corrected by the present editor. Deleted text is enclosed in pointed brackets. No account is made of superscript letters not so printed by Stead. The marks of punctuation and the distinction between capital and minuscule letters in the original manuscript are so frequently ambiguous that it has not seemed worth while to record the occasions where my reading varies from Stead's in these matters.

Five errata in the text of Stead's edition were corrected by him in a slip inserted in most copies. Not all copies of his book contain the slip, so these are included in the table with appropriate comment.

The letters *MS* identify a reading in the original manuscript, the letter *S* a reading in Stead's edition. The editor's comments are printed in italics, the text and its variants in roman type.

JUBILATE AGNO

FRAGMENT A

Line

10 set him at large] let him at large *S, corrected in errata-slip.*
14 Naphtali] Naphthali *MS, S.*
16 y^e *appears to be a later insertion in MS.*
19 Pygarg] Pygarg [Hart] *S; in MS.* Hart. *is written in Smart's hand above* Pygarg *in a different ink.*
41 hand] hanp *overwritten to read* hand *in MS.*
    sweetness magnifical] sweetness ⟨majestic and⟩ magnifical *MS.*
42 the glory] the the glory *MS, S.*
78 Azariah] Azarias *MS, S.*
94 of the tree] of tree *MS, S.*

FRAGMENT B1, LET VERSES

6 the *careted in MS.*
24 Hillel] Hilleb *S.*
31 signet of God] sight of God *S.*
33 Jamin] Jamim *MS, S.*
41 Ziphion] Ziphien *S.*
42 their number] there number *MS, S.*
59 its] it's *MS.*
80 Japhia] Japhua *MS, S.*
89 falconry] falonry *MS.*
94 armour-bearer rejoice with] armour-bearer with *MS; Stead's emendation.*
103 its] it's *MS, S.*
109 Ibzan] Ibzam *MS, S.*
123 MOON FISH] MOONFISH *S.*
128 Bartholomew] Bartholemew *MS, S.*
157 blessd] blessed *S.*
161 Bartimæus] Bartimeus *MS, S.*
163 Timæus] Timeus *MS, S.*
203 mother of James] mother James *MS; Stead's emendation.*
263 to Mr FLETCHER] to I Mr FLETCHER *S; in MS the* I *appears to be a false start for* F.
265 Erastus] Erastis *S.*
266 murder'd—] murder'd ⟨by Atterbury⟩—*MS.*
274 Silvanus] Sylvanus *MS, S.*
275 O Tite siquid ego adjuero curamve levasso!] O Tite si quid ego adjuero curam ve levasso! *S.*
285 Onesiphorus] Onesephorus *MS, S.*
291 Zenas] Zemas *MS, S.*

FRAGMENT B1, FOR VERSES

3 For my existimation] For in my existimation *S; in MS,* in *has been erased and is barely visible.*

TEXTUAL NOTES

4   such as are] such are *MS; Stead's emendation.*
9   without] withot *MS.*
54   *MS in this line contains three deletions, which do not entirely yield to visual examination, or ultra-violet or infra-red photography. The approximate length of the unreadable portions is indicated by dots:* For ⟨. . . . .⟩ Agricola ⟨. . . . . .⟩ is Γηωργος ⟨which is by the blessing of God SAINT GEORGE⟩. *S reads* Γεωργος.
58   For CHRISTOPHER] For ⟨Agricola is SAINT GEORGE, but his son⟩ CHRISTOPHER *MS.*
      PHEON's head] PAEON's head *S.*
120   For the adversary] For the th adversary *MS.*
170   built] bluilt *MS, S.*
194   Sʳ] Sir *S.*
196   constituents] constinuents *MS, S.*
207   For there is] For is *MS, S.*
      but] *careted in MS.*
227   figure is compleat] figure compleat *MS; Stead's emendation.*
228   HIMSELF] HIMSLF *MS,* HIMS[E]LF *S.*
243   BENJAMIN] BENJIMIN *MS.*
244   instruments] instrument *MS, S.*
251   will be known] be *is careted in MS.*
252   LITURGY] LITURTY *MS,* LITURTY [liturgy] *S.*
258   For nothing is] For is *MS; Stead's emendation.*
266   may be exasperated] may exasperated *MS; Stead's emendation.*
268   philosophizing] philosopizing *MS, S.*
282   & I overcame] & overcame *MS; Stead's emendation.*
290   not at all] not all *MS; Stead's emendation.*
292   of wicked men] of wicked of men *MS, S.*
294   of Heaven shall] of Heaven of shall *MS, S.*

FRAGMENT B2

299   Witchcraft] Wh Witchcraft *MS, S.*
300   witches] witchces *MS, S.*
324   God bring] God be bring *MS, S.*
331   beyond] beyong *MS, S.*
333   being] beeing *MS, S.*
374   SQUARED] SQARED *MS, S.*
376   no rain] no ⟨ain⟩ rain *MS,* no ain rain *S.*
382   the MILLENNIUM of] the MILLENIUM of *MS, S.*
386   says] *careted in MS.*
396   Locke] Lock *MS, S.*
399   Moabites] moabites *MS.*
404   punching] *this word is emphasized in MS.*
      reader] *the letter* a *is careted in MS.*

JUBILATE AGNO

412   constituent] constinuent *MS.*
      stones] stone *MS, S.*
419   Sodom] Sodam *MS, S.*
424   this was inverting] this inverting *MS, S.*
427   skin?' the] skin? the *MS, S.*
429   God is upon] God upon *MS, S.*
453   For] L *is written under* F *in MS, as if Smart mistakenly began to write* Let.
459   destruction of books] destruction books *MS; Stead's emendation.*
470   preperation] preparation *S.*
471   sovereign] sovereing *MS, S.*
473   murderers] murderes *MS,* murdere[r]s *S.*
474   withheld] witheld *MS, S.*
482   in] *careted in MS.*
485   upon all] upon on all *MS, S.*
495   carried it] it *inserted in minute characters in MS.*
537   of children] *careted in MS.*
577   The Golden fleece] the Golden the fleece *MS, S.*
597   has its marrow] has it marrow *MS, S.*
610   Gad] God, *S, corrected in errata-slip.*
635   line] lines *S.*
674   with earning] with [y]earning *S.*
686   painted] paited *MS.*
701   musk] s *written over* c *in MS.*
709   fifthly] fiftly *MS, S.*
712   Eighthly] Eightly *S.*
717   give it a chance] give it chance *MS; Stead's emendation.*
720   For he keeps] For keeps *MS, S.*

FRAGMENT C, LET VERSES

7   Chephirah] Chepirah *S.*
11   Senaah] Senach *S.*
20   Sophereth] *altered from a longer word by erasure in MS.*
31–32 *S reads:*
      Let Hagab rejoice with Serpyllum Mother of Thyme. Hosanna to the
         memory of Q. Anne. March 8th. NS 1761.
      Let Shalmai rejoice with Meadow Rue.—E
         God be gracious to old Windsmore.
      What S reads as E *is actually a brace used to set apart the run-over line*
         31 *in MS.*
46   Mithredath] Mithridath *MS, S.*
70   Ferula] Terula *S; but S correctly reads* Ferula *in his note on the line.*
74   Zebina] Zebida *MS, S.*
76   Jadau] Jadan *S.*
80   Jeziah] Jeriah *S.*
88   Shashai] Shasai *S.*

TEXTUAL NOTES

Line

99   Henadad] Henadiad *MS, S; the* i *is a later insertion in MS.*
100 Shallum] Shallun *MS, S.*
104 to the house] to house *MS, S.*
138 Son of Pahath-moab] Son Pahath-moab *MS; Stead's emendation.*
143 Ginnethon] Ginnithon *MS, S.*
154 Beninu] Benina *MS, S.*
157 Hizkijah] Hiskijah *MS, S.*

FRAGMENT C, FOR VERSES

43   not] *careted in MS.*
45   be] *careted in MS.*
46   ת] ח *S, corrected in errata-slip.*
     letter in the] letter of the *S.*
55   the harp in] *careted in MS.*
56   sustaind] sustained *S.*
65   there] *careted in MS.*
     be] *careted in MS.*
80   this is a] this a *MS; Stead's emendation.*
     communicating of God] communicating God *MS, S.*
85   according to the] according the *MS; Stead's emendation.*
86   grace] *MS shows signs of erasure under this word.*
114 they] *careted in MS.*
119 Man] Men *MS, S; S emends in errata-slip.*
159 For it is] For is *MS; Stead's emendation.*

FRAGMENT D

51   herb—gem] herb—germ *S, corrected in errata-slip.*
75   —very likely.] *a later addition in MS.*
77   Gloucester] Glouscester *MS, S.*
82   Not so . . . word.] *appears to be a later addition in MS.*
92   are] are are *MS, S.*
118 Trigonum] Trigonium *S.*
124 Condurdon] Condurden *S.*
125 care for my cough] care my cough *MS;* care [cure?] my cough *S.*
129 11. Let Mace] 10. Let Mace *S.*
130 an herb] a herb *S.*
144 & his] and his *S.*
153 grashopper] grasshopper *S.*
155 Let Brecknock] Let Breckock *MS;* Let Breck[n]ock *S.*
156 Purslaine] Purslain *S.*
     & family] and family *S.*
158 shou'd] should *S.*
160 & his] and his *S.*
165 & family] and family *S.*

169

JUBILATE AGNO

Line
170 Græcula] Graecula *S.*
171 Hadrosphærum] Hadrosphaerum *S.*
    a kind] kind *MS; Stead's emendation.*
172 Hæmotimon] Haemotimon *S.*
188 Beardmanica] Beard manica *S.*
198 the whole University] the whose University *MS.*
223 consider] considere *MS, S.*
224 Kinleside] Kirleside *S; but S correctly reads* Kinleside *in his note on the
    line.*

CONVERSION TABLE

To convert a line number in the present edition to its equivalent in Stead's edition, subtract the appropriate conversion factor in the centre column of this table; to reverse the process, add the factor.

Present Edition Fragment: Line.	Conversion Factor	Stead's Edition Section: Line.
A: 1	(0)	I: 1
A: 26	(±25)	II: 1
A: 56	(±55)	III: 1
A: 86	(±85)	IV: 1
Let B1: 1	(0)	V: 1
Let B1: 71	(±70)	VI: 1
Let B1: 151	(±150)	XIII: 1
Let B1: 222	(±221)	XIV: 1
For B1: 1	(0)	VII: 1
For B1: 71	(±70)	VIII: 1
For B1: 151	(±150)	IX: 1
For B1: 222	(±221)	X: 1
B2: 296	(±295)	XI: 1
B2: 363	(±362)	XII: 1
B2: 411	(±410)	XV: 1
B2: 453	(±452)	XVI: 1
B2: 513	(±512)	XVII: 1
B2: 583	(±582)	XVIII :1
B2: 647	(±646)	XIX: 1
B2: 707	(±706)	XX: 1
Let C: 1	(0)	XXI: 1
Let C: 81	(±80)	XXII: 1
For C: 1	(0)	XXIII: 1
For C: 81	(±80)	XXIV: 1
D: 1	(0)	XXV: 1
D: 33	(±32)	XXVI: 1
D: 65	(±64)	XXVII: 1
D: 97	(±96)	XXVIII: 1
D: 129	(±128)	XXIX: 1
D: 162	(±161)	XXX: 1
D: 195	(±194)	XXXI: 1
D: 230	(±229)	XXXII: 1